WEYMOUTH

WEYMOUTH

New Chronicles AND OLD YARNS FROM THE SOUTH SHORE

TED CLARKE

THE History PRESS

Published by The History Press
Charleston, SC 29403
www.historypress.net

First published 2009

Manufactured in the United States

ISBN 978.1.59629.845.3

Library of Congress Cataloging-in-Publication Data

Clarke, Theodore G.
Weymouth : new chronicles and old yarns from the South Shore / Ted Clarke.
p. cm.
ISBN 978-1-59629-845-3
1. Weymouth (Mass.)--History. I. Title.
F74.W77C53 2009
974.4'7--dc22
2009038610

CONTENTS

PART I

The Early Days

Weymouth Prehistory

History is really a story of places, people and events that connect with one another. If we can find the connections, the story has meaning.

In telling the story of Weymouth, we use connections to join past and present and give us a clear picture of what happened in this South Shore town.

We all like to think that we have common sense, and common sense tells us that the location and geography of Weymouth make it a natural place for people to want to live and work. History tells us that we're right. People have, in fact, lived here for a long time.

People lived in Weymouth one thousand years ago and probably further back than that. The natives who lived here didn't keep written records, but history has other ways of telling its story. We know that people lived in the area because historians have found artifacts that date back that far.

The big discovery was a dugout canoe, found in Great Pond in South Weymouth in 1965. That was the year that a big drought ravaged Massachusetts, and the huge pond had become shallow, particularly along its edges. Some boys playing near the pond uncovered the wooden canoe, and Chester Kevitt, town historian, had it brought to Tufts Library (where it still is). Carbon-14 testing showed that it was about six hundred years old.

This was a spectacular find, and it kindled the curiosity of those who wonder about how things came to be and how other people lived in earlier times. This curiosity is one of the God-given gifts that let us advance as individuals and groups, and the people in Weymouth were clearly blessed with it.

Naturally, locating such a find from the past made the people from the twentieth century wonder about their predecessors and persuaded them to look around more carefully. But where should they look? Well, the canoe gave a clue. These natives must have lived around the ponds and rivers. They probably fished there, too. The ponds and rivers of Weymouth connect with one another and lead to the sea, so the Indians must have spent lots of time there and probably left things behind from time to time.

Sure enough, other Indian artifacts were also found, mainly around the ponds and streams of the town. Some of them were even older than the canoe—*thousands* of years older in some cases. Those who were curious pieced together the clues they had from native culture and learned that a group called the Massachusetts lived in what is now Weymouth—or at least they spent some of their time there, mostly in the summer when they fished. They had more permanent dwellings in the more thickly wooded Blue Hills south and west of there, but their hunting, fishing and gathering took them to the waterways of what the white settlers would later call "Weymouth" and especially to the shores of North Weymouth, where they had a small village they called "Wessagusset."

This was where they first encountered white men, but as things turned out, a disease had thinned the native ranks just a few years before settlers arrived in 1622. It had killed many Indians near the coast of Massachusetts and around Massachusetts Bay. That event had something to do with the choice of Weymouth for settlement.

"SPARROW" HOPPING

Why did the English colonists come to New England in the first place? Why did they choose Wessagusset? How did they get along with the natives? We have answers to each of those questions, but other ones remain a mystery.

A Londoner named Thomas Weston was the prime mover in all of this, but he was not a typical settler. When we think of early New England, we're likely to picture the sternly religious Pilgrims and Puritans who came to America for religious freedom.

Weston, though, was not cut from that cloth. Religion was not his thing. The notion of setting up colonies for future generations did not have much appeal for him, either. Making money made Weston's bell ring. He was what they called a "merchant-adventurer." He had already dipped his toe into the salty waters of the Atlantic by helping to finance the Pilgrims and paying part of the cost of the *Mayflower*'s trip. But Weston didn't do that because he was a nice guy. He expected a payback. He wanted the Pilgrim settlers to send timber, beaver skins and fish back to England.

Just as Weston didn't care much about religion, so did the Pilgrims care little about trade. They didn't provide Weston with the things he demanded, and it wasn't long before he lost interest in them. When he made additional demands on them, the partnership fizzled out. He sold his shares in the Plymouth Company in May 1622. But Weston still believed that a New England settlement could make money, so he decided to form his own company and his own settlement.

He obtained a grant to six thousand acres of land in Massachusetts Bay and bought two ships, the *Charity* and the *Swan*, as well as a smaller vessel, the *Sparrow*. Weston had learned about the New England coast from those who had been there.

Stories and maps can only tell you so much, though. Weston sent the *Sparrow* to New England early in 1622 to check things out. It stopped first at the fishing station along the Maine coast, and from there a few men took a smaller boat, called a shallop, to explore the coast. They were looking for a good place for a trading post, and they found an excellent area along the Fore River in Massachusetts Bay called "Wessagusset" in the Indian tongue spoken there. But by then the epidemics had wiped out most of the population a few years before. Not having large numbers of Indians around was all right with this group.

The traders also liked this area for the reasons previously mentioned: it was located on the coast but was protected; it had rivers with inlets and power; and there were fish and shellfish. It also had marsh grass that could be harvested and open lands that could be settled without their having to go to the trouble of cutting down lots of trees.

They then agreed that this would be the location for their trading post. They continued south to Plymouth to join the rest of their company.

Meanwhile, Weston had sent over his two other ships, the *Charity* and the *Swan*. They reached Plymouth in June. The *Charity* went on to Virginia, while a few of the sixty to seventy men in the *Swan*, led by Weston's brother-in-law, Richard Greene, left for Wessagusset, where they were welcomed by the Indians and their sachem Aberdecest. They exchanged gifts and made arrangements with the Indians to give them the right to settle there. They chose a site for their settlement where the Fore River makes a left turn toward the south, a place later called Hunt's Hill.

The location was described as land that projected into the water, with a curving point. When they passed around it, they came to what was described as a beautiful bay sheltered from wind and waves. Here they anchored and stepped ashore.

History is often uncertain. Documents are lost and accounts vary. People interpret the same data differently. We find several cases like that in the history of Weymouth. One of them is a long-standing doubt about where Weston's men landed. In 1884, a map of Massachusetts Bay drawn by Governor Winthrop in 1634 was located, and this map actually *shows* the site of the Weston settlement at Hunt's Hill between the present location of the Fore River Bridge and the foot of Sea Street. The "beautiful bay" would have been what we call King's Cove. It was undoubtedly more beautiful then.

Hunt's Hill (top left) and North Weymouth.

The name John Smith is usually associated with Jamestown, Virginia, and in some chronicles he appears as a troublemaker. He was, in fact, a daring adventurer, a soldier of fortune and an expert mapmaker and writer of travelogues. His map and account of Weymouth gave inspiration to Thomas Weston. He also had a map made by Smith in 1614, which included Boston Bay and what is now Weymouth. Smith had described the region as the "Paradise of New England." So he certainly agreed with Winthrop's assessment of the "beautiful bay."

Local tradition (backed by maps) had it that it was on Hunt's Hill (which is no longer there) that the settlers built a blockhouse for protection. The houses and the other buildings they needed were built nearby. In the summer of 2009, the Town of Weymouth received a report it had commissioned that included an archaeological study and an appraisal of the available history of the area around Hunt's Hill. This report suggested that the settlement may have been located a little farther south than had been supposed but also said that more written evidence was needed.

It seems clear that the first English settlement was located near or in King's Cove. As the Fore River flows through North Weymouth from Boston Harbor, it does take a left turn south at Hunt's Hill. The first stretch of this is cut by inlets and coves, and even now there's a shipyard in this well-protected area.

Protection was one of the keys that made Wessagusset appealing to Weston's men. It was and is a good place to dock wooden sailing ships without worrying about having them dashed to splinters on the rocks. The area had two fast-moving and navigable rivers, a wall of islands to keep ocean storm surges away and an abundance of fish and shellfish, as well as marsh grass and seaweed that could be harvested and packed along the foundations of houses for insulation. Both the Fore River and the Back River were deep enough for sailing ships, and each had some rapid or falling water that could be used for power, but they also had protected inlets at which you could tie up a boat or build a mill or fishery.

Settlement and Conflict

Those of Weston's men who had been left in Plymouth went on to Wessagusset in the late summer of 1622, and they were indeed all men—no women and no families. That was what Weston wanted. They were said to number thirty servants and thirty gentlemen, but both the number and the type of men is questionable. What is certain is that these men were *not* prepared to be colonists. They did not know how to take care of themselves in an undeveloped land. In particular, they failed to provide a storehouse of food for the cold weather to come. They existed hand-to-mouth, using up the fish and other food they acquired and saving nothing for later on. They built a fort and huts, but they had no skills and no provisions for hunting, planting or fishing.

You'll remember that the Pilgrims had Squanto to teach them these things. Squanto was a unique find. A homeless Indian who was educated in London and spoke perfect English, he understood the Pilgrims' needs, interpreted for other Indians and showed the settlers how to survive. Weston's men had no such help. Some starved. In "A Voyage to New England" (written at that time), Christopher Levett said that they went about to build "Castles in the Aire." His opinion may have been on solid ground.

This group was expected to establish a trading post but failed. However, it was only the first of three consecutive groups that came close to overlapping one another, but each wave was an improvement on the last, and these early settlers established several fine traditions, some of which continue today.

For example, early Weymouth settlers make for an excellent example of a group of people who formed their own rules and laws, governed themselves and took advantage of the things they found at this inlet of Massachusetts Bay. The first group that settled there was not the one that made these things happen. The settlers did locate an excellent spot for the town to grow, but they were not prepared to get along with their neighbors, take care of themselves or leave a heritage for those who came after. From the second group of settlers, only a few had a major impact on the future town. But both of these groups left an ember of life that grew into a colonial settlement and then a town. The resilience and self-reliance of these early people led to the Weymouth we know today.

These people weren't just names in a history book, though. They were human beings just like us. So, like us, they did some things well and some things poorly. When they came up against problems, they couldn't search the Internet or get on the phone for a solution. They had to find their own. Let's take a look at how the early settlers succeeded and how they failed, and let's see how the town built upon these early foundations.

The first problem to hit the original wave of settlers was hunger. Such pangs let you know quickly and clearly that you need to have food, and Weston's men had no idea how to grow it and were not skilled fishermen either.

Once they realized that they were in trouble, the Wessagusset men joined with the Plymouth settlers for some foraging and trading expeditions, and they did bring home some food. By late winter, though, they ran out again. They then turned to the Indians, and here again they failed in their dealings. They traded for corn, giving up clothes and blankets or performing services for them like cutting wood.

The Indians didn't think much of men who would do these things and couldn't take care of themselves, so this did not gain the settlers respect, and when some of them began to steal corn from the Indians, things got worse.

One man was caught stealing corn that belonged to natives, and the Indians demanded that the white settlers punish him. (The punishment would have been hanging.) However, the thief was a tall, strong young man, one of their best workers and a cobbler, too—in a place and time where having adequate footwear was essential. He was, therefore, very valuable to them.

They held a trial. Some of the settlers wanted to take a sickly, dying weaver, dress him in the clothes of the thief and hang *him* instead. But in the end (if you accept the version that I do) the true thief was hanged. If he was not, it was a bad start for justice in America. Whomever they hanged, it did not settle the problem.

The current leader at Wessagusset, John Saunders, wanted to steal food from the Indians, but the people of Plymouth talked him out of it. He then left for the Maine fishing villages by shallop to get food there but was not heard from again at Wessagusset. We now know that Saunders stayed in Maine. After that, food became even more scarce. In all, ten settlers died through hardship or disease.

Relations between the settlers and natives were now at their darkest point. What happened after that varies from one account to the next.

This is the most logical and most reliable version, but you should know that others exist.

The natives, particularly one called Wituwaumet and one called Pecksuot, either threatened or appeared to be threatening not only the Wessagusset settlers but those of Plymouth, too. There had recently been a massacre of settlers by Indians in Virginia, and news of this event had reached the settlers at Wessagusset and Plymouth, as well as the Indians of the area. As you can imagine, that made the settlers jittery and more wary of Indians. The news may also have emboldened the Indians, who had been afraid of the firearms the white settlers carried.

Phineas Pratt, now a leader of the Wessagusset contingent, believed from the actions of the Indians that they were planning an attack. He expected an attack to take place both there and at Plymouth and that it would begin when the snow melted.

Pratt made up his mind that he would go to Plymouth on foot by night to warn them. In the account he left for us, he says that he was followed by an Indian but eluded his pursuer by staying out of snow and mud, where he would have left tracks.

As it turned out, his trip made no difference because the Pilgrims had already heard of the plan for an attack from the sachem Massasoit. The chief had told a Plymouth settler who had treated him for an illness.

Those in Plymouth believed what Massasoit relayed to them and were prepared to make a preemptive strike. They had already heard bad things about the Indians at Wessagusset and planned to send Myles Standish and eight other men by boat to Wessagusset. Standish had met Wituwaumet earlier and had considered some of the Indian's words to him to be threatening and insulting, so he was ready to take action. According to one version, when he arrived, Wituwaumet and Pecksuot visited Standish inside the stockade, where Wituwaumet warned of destruction and the two Indians taunted the small but well-built Standish about his short stature.

The next day, April 6, 1623, brought the decisive struggle. Somehow Standish lured Pecksuot, Wituwaumet and some others into the stockade, apparently for a feast. Five whites and four Indians were present. Standish had hoped for more Indians, but the two strongest fighters were there so he proceeded with his plan.

At a signal, the doors were closed, and Standish grabbled Pecksuot and got the big Indian's knife out of its sheath. The two wrestled with it, but Standish finally prevailed, killing Pecksuot with his own knife.

Wituwaumet was also killed, as was one other Indian, and the remainder of the Indians were routed. Wituwaumet was beheaded, and his head was taken to Plymouth, where it was stuck on a pike and displayed at the fort as a warning, as was an English custom of that time.

Historian Charles Francis Adams, who took a keen interest in Wessagusset, believed that the preemptive attack saved not only Wessagusset, but Plymouth as well, since the larger tribes may well have joined in against both groups.

Adams also bemoans (as do today's historians) the loss of historic Hunt's Hill, which was thoughtlessly sold for gravel to be used on the causeway between South Boston and Castle Island in 1874.

This was the end, though, of the first wave of settlement. Standish had to return to Plymouth, and most of the Wessagusset settlers went there or to the fishing stations on the Maine coast. According to Pratt, three settlers remained at Wessagusset and were killed by the Indians.

Wessagusset Becomes Weymouth

All of this action took place in North Weymouth, somewhere southeast of Hunt's Hill, where a stockade had been built, most likely at the corner of the present Ocean and Birchbrow Avenues.

To the southeast of Hunt's Hill was Hunt's Plain. The two were separated by a ravine (often called a "sneak-through") used by Indians. Hunt's Hill was the base in the early 1700s of a joint stock company in the fishing trade. As of 1876, it was the location of a shipyard operated by N. Porter Keene after the hill had been sold for landfill. The history of this early period is recalled in many of the street names in North Weymouth: Pecksuot, Wituwaumet, Standish, Hobomock and, of course, Wessagusset.

Shadows of the past return, however. Two headless skeletons uncovered near the foot of Sea Street are believed to be those of Pecksuot and Wituwaumet. The skeletons were unearthed in the early 1800s, when the cellar was dug for a house at 236 Sea Street. These bones were kindly interred in the tomb of the owner of that house (Edward Blanchard) at North Cemetery.

In 1930, workers digging a hole for a flagpole at the Bicknell School in Bicknell Square uncovered the skeleton of a papoose with its head bashed in and later an Indian squaw's skeleton with the skull in the same condition. It has been speculated that these were the wife and child of the Weston settler known to have taken an Indian wife.

In the early 1900s, a house was built over the tomb of the first colony at 43 Bicknell Road, near the Fore River. Seven skulls were found. The owners placed five of the seven skulls into a wall in the cellar, but these were later removed and the empty spaces filled with cement. A 2009 study showed five "anomalies" deep in the wall where the skulls had once been placed.

A later owner of the house and her children, who had just moved to Weymouth and knew nothing of the town's history or the mystery surrounding the house, reported being awakened at night to see what she believed to be the ghost of a giant Indian (Pecksuot?) glowering at them.

In September 1623, less than six months after the killings at the blockhouse, the buildings on the site were again occupied by English settlers intent on starting a trading post and colony.

This time their leader was Captain Robert Gorges, son of Sir Fernando Gorges, the New England explorer of earlier years. Robert Gorges brought with him several families, and he also held a grant from the government. Curiously, although they sailed from Weymouth, England, they didn't plan to come to Wessagusset. About 120 passengers, including both men and women, sailed in two ships, the *Katherine* and the *Prophet Daniel*. They planned to start a colony farther north and might well have wound up in Boston but for storms with heavy crosswinds that made them put in and take shelter at Wessagusset, which we know—and they probably did, too—is well protected from storms.

They easily settled in, using the abandoned buildings and adding others to house their large group. Two ministers ordained by the Church of England were with them—Reverends William Morell and William Blaxton. Morell did not stay long, but Blaxton would soon become the first white man to settle in Boston.

Robert Gorges didn't stay long in America. His father back in England sent him a message telling him to come home. There had been bad financial and political news affecting the family. Gorges and some of his settlers returned to England in the spring of 1624. But some of the Gorges group, along with some of the Weston people who had been in Plymouth, continued the unbroken settlement of Wessagusset.

Others left Wessagusset later. Reverend Morell went back to England in 1625, and Reverend Blaxton (or Blackstone), as mentioned, became the first white settler of Boston until the Puritans arrived. Samuel Maverick (who arrived with Gorges) built a house at Winnisimmet, which is now Chelsea, and later was granted Noddle's Island (East Boston). Thomas Morton, who had been in Wessagusset and returned to England, settled Mount Wollaston (later Braintree and now Quincy).

There were enough people remaining at Wessagusset to perpetuate the colony, and others arrived in small numbers over the next several years. Meanwhile, other settlements were being forged along the coast of Massachusetts, including at Cape Ann and Dorchester. Salem was settled by a Puritan group in 1628 and Boston by another in 1630.

By the time Boston was settled, about three hundred people were living in and around the settlement at Wessagusset. At that time, Wessagusset was recognized as part of the Massachusetts Bay Colony, seated at Boston, and in 1632 Governor Winthrop of Boston visited Weymouth on his way south.

A visit from a politician isn't always good news, and during the same year that the governor visited, a tax was levied by the General Court at Boston. Wessagusset had to pay five pounds (as opposed to eight for Boston and four for Salem).

The settlement expanded steadily. The infusion of population was such that it soon became a plantation called "Weymouth." There were sufficient numbers who had originated in Weymouth, England, to make that name a logical choice. In 1635, Wessagusset became incorporated as Weymouth. In that year, Reverend Joseph Hull came from Weymouth, England, on the *Assurance* with twenty-one families and was given permission by Massachusetts Bay Colony in Boston to reside in Weymouth. By that time, it had become clear that enough people were arriving to ensure a permanent settlement.

The first representative to the General Court (legislature) in Boston was named William Reade, a tailor. Many prominent families of today's Weymouth had ancestors among the Hull Company.

One of the unique facts about early Weymouth was that it was governed by the people themselves. Unlike Plymouth, Boston and Salem, all of which had governors, Weymouth had none. All decisions were made by the settlers gathering together town meeting style. That type of town government has continued to the present day in many places in New England, but it all started in Weymouth when it was incorporated as a town in 1635. It is also the "spiritual grandfather" of the town hall meetings that gained prominence in the summer of 2009.

According to historian Charles Francis Adams, "[F]or those Towns there was no prophet, no chief, no lord, no bishop, no King. Those dwelling in them were all plain people. They stood on their own legs, such as they were; and there was no one to hold them up."

The next year, boundaries were set, with Quincy (then "Mt. Wollaston") using the Fore River and Smelt Brook, and with Hingham (then "Bare Cove") using the Back River and Fresh River. Grape Island and Round Island were made part of Weymouth.

In 1635, Thomas Applegate of Weymouth was licensed to run a ferry between Wessagusset and Mount Wollaston. The boat was used to transfer salt, which was taken from the marshes. Marsh grass was also dried and used to thatch roofs of the huts. Seaweed was useful, too. The early settlers packed it along the base of their houses to keep out the cold in winter.

OLD SPAIN

The early settlers not only fished and gathered shellfish, they also raised grains and vegetables and kept animals. Since the area was wooded, lumber made for a good business. The rivers and harbors made it possible to dock ships and send the lumber to other places. But as trees became scarce, laws had to be made about cutting them down.

Most of the early history of Weymouth took place in North Weymouth, once called "Old Spain." In this book, past and present are brought together by working from places of historical significance and other public places within the town.

Perhaps the best place to appreciate what the early settlers saw and foresaw is from the top of the glacial drumlin known as Great Hill. The fast-moving water at the foot of the hill with the oceangoing traffic is Fore River. Across it lies the small city of Quincy, and beyond that towers the city of Boston about ten miles distant.

To the right, or east, is Back River, and beyond it the town of Hingham. A ring of harbor islands and the peninsula of Hull provide the protection from the ocean that impressed visitors in the early 1600s.

The place where the first settlers dropped anchor lies less than a mile to the west, where the Fore River turns the corner into King's Cove. We

Above: View from Great Hill, North Weymouth.

Below: Bicknell Square.

Above: Wessagusset Gardens.

Below: Edgar Edison Station.

can easily drive there by descending the hill to Sea Street and turning right. At the second traffic light you will have entered Bicknell Square. The building with the wide driveway on the left is the former Bicknell School, where the skeletons of the squaw and papoose were found.

Turn right on Sea Street, and as you approach Fore River you will pass a wooded area with signs and monuments popularly known as Wessagusset Gardens, which has historic significance. Just past that and on a rise is the Blanchard House, where two headless skeletons were found.

If you take the trail into the wooded area, you will see a house on a hill on the riverside. This is the mysterious House of Skulls at 43 Bicknell Road.

If you continue to the river and turn left onto Fore River Avenue, you will reach the intersection with Birchbrow Avenue, where the blockhouse reportedly stood. Hunt's Hill is gone and so is the N. Porter Keene Shipyard, but the inlet behind the houses on Birchbrow is still known as King's Cove. You can get a better view of the waterfront by continuing to Route 3A and turning right just at the foot of the Fore River Bridge. Here is a new park with fine views.

Drive under the bridge and you will see an energy plant that replaced the huge Edgar Edison Station, long a South Shore landmark. On that same site in the late nineteenth century was a popular amusement park called Lovell's Grove that had hotels, rides and regular ferry service to Boston and Quincy.

If you head south on Route 3A and return to Bicknell Square, taking a right onto Sea Street, you will enter one of the oldest parts of Weymouth. The oldest house in town is the 1650 Bicknell House, which is located second on the right (number 82). It once served as a shoe factory, as well as a home. On its right is the former home of Dr. Wallace Drake, one of the founders of the South Shore Hospital.

Still on that side but across from the post office is the site of the Elias Beals shoe factory, first to use the sewing machine. Beals also represented the town in the state legislature, and it was he who got the tolls lifted from both the Quincy and Hingham ends of Bridge Street. He also donated the land for Beals Park, which is located behind the post office.

The Italianate house at number 22 is the Thomas House. It was built in 1783, the year the Revolution ended. Next to it, the funeral home was once the Matthewson House.

Above: Beals Factory, Sea Street.

Below: Thomas Corner, Sea North Streets.

Number 10 Sea Street was the waiting station for trolleys, and the shop next to it was the post office. The intersection with North was called Thomas Corner, and the whole area has been listed by the National Park Service as the Sea Street National Historic District.

Shaw Street meets North at the North Library. Turning right from it onto Green Street, you come to the former home of Matthew Pratt II. It's the third-oldest house in town and is a saltbox Cape Cod–style building. The garage was used as a blacksmith shop until 1940. Inside are four original fireplaces that warmed the house during New England winters. The fireplaces all used a common chimney. Cape chimneys of that era were usually the only ways to heat the colonial home. In Capes of that period the chimney was typically located in the center of the house. This fireplace also has a beehive oven, common during the late seventeenth century.

Those houses were built to be protected from the weather. Families retired when the sun went down and rose when it did. There were few means of entertainment, and in fact, early settlers owned few things except for the furniture. For that reason and because there wasn't much space, these homes didn't have closets as we know them. Storage spaces were built wherever there was room, as in areas around the fireplace.

Green Street turns into Neck, which meets Bridge Street—Route 3A. A right turn will lead you toward Hingham. Before coming to Great Esker Park, one can see a shopping plaza built on the land that was once the Weymouth Drive-in Theatre. It was one of the first drive-in movie theatres in the country and the first in New England. It boasted the world's largest screen at that time.

Churches and Government

Although the first settlers brought no clergy, subsequent groups did. Early church records show that the first church was "gathered" on Watch Hill (where North Cemetery is now). A more permanent building was built in 1682. But the several Protestant sects in town did not get along, and things became so heated that by 1642 some forty families had moved to Rehoboth on the Rhode Island border near where William Blaxton (formerly of Wessagusset and Boston) was now living. Others such as Roger Williams and Ann Hutchinson, driven out of Boston by the Puritans, also migrated to the Rhode Island area. Blaxton said that he left England to "get away from the power of the Lord's Bishops, but he left Boston to get away from the power of the Lord's Brethren."

Two Indian wars affected Weymouth during its first decades. The Pequot War came in 1637 and drew five soldiers from Weymouth. In that same year, the Massachusetts General Court (legislature) issued an order to protect towns from Indian attack. It said that no houses could be built more than a half-mile from the church. But Weymouth had already spread as far as Whitman's Pond, far more distant than a half-mile.

Weymouth was already governing itself. Since the first days, decisions were made by all the men in a single gathering, but formal records of town meetings began in 1641. The year after that, title to the land was purchased from the Indians. As of 1651, two town meetings per year were required.

However, it can be fun to look at early records to get a picture of how things were. Examination of early town meeting records shows that human nature has not really changed over the years, judging from the various complaints against people for violating their neighbors' rights or the laws that townspeople had made collectively.

The records also show how the town was run. For example, the church and town were clearly joined—not separated—as shown from a 1682 vote to form a committee to consider whether to repair or replace the old meetinghouse (church). The committee took only three weeks to recommend replacement due to rotting wood and the need for more space and light. People at the town meeting agreed with their recommendation, and the work began at once. Though human nature may be the same, this kind of speed in government action may be a "thing of the past."

A bigger and wider Indian war began in 1675. It was known as King Philip's War, and Weymouth was attacked. On February 12, 1675, several houses were burned in the center of town where Washington and Middle Streets now meet. Some settlers were killed. The following year, houses and barns were burned in a raid, and one month later a Weymouth resident was killed in an attack. Even when they were not under attack, residents lived in fear because many of their men were away fighting along the Connecticut River.

Tradition has it that fights between settlers and Indians took place on White's Neck (now Idelwell) near Mill Creek, at the base of Cemetery Hill, near the Great Swamp on Neck Street and one on Middle Street near Whitman's Pond.

Not only were there religious separations, but there was also a rift between South Weymouth and the rest of town. With a town as many miles long as Weymouth (nine), it was difficult to get from one end to the other, particularly when the roads were nothing more than rutted paths and especially when the weather got bad. But everybody was expected to be at the meetinghouse in the north end of town every Sabbath and holy day.

In 1721, a second meetinghouse was built in the south part of town. Naturally, a church required a minister, and a minister required a salary. And who should pay for him? The town was paying for the minister in the north of town, but the people who lived there didn't see why they should pay for a second one in the south. It wasn't in their backyard.

The south then petitioned the Massachusetts General Court to become a new precinct or township. The north opposed it, but the second precinct was created in 1723, and a minister was appointed.

In 1751, a fire destroyed the first church, located on the hill at Weymouth Heights. It was replaced, and the congregation continued to worship together. The current structure dates to 1833 and is the third building to stand on the Church Street location.

Church fires are not uncommon. Often, the spires themselves have been targets of lightning. Unattended buildings frequently burn beyond recall before help can be summoned. There have been several church fires in Weymouth, each with a follow-up.

The Union Church of Weymouth and Braintree at Weymouth Landing was erected in 1810 and totally destroyed by sparks from a train locomotive in 1897. While a historic landmark was lost, the church bought land around the corner in Braintree and built the current building the next year.

The "Old South" in Columbian Square was destroyed by fire in 1989 and was replicated by the current building exactly two years later. The cost of this replication—with its interior updates—indicates the financial difficulties. The original building was built in 1853–54 for $15, 250. The current building cost $3.8 million. Nonetheless, the Old South Union Congregational Church continues on Columbian Street. It carries on the history of the second precinct.

The most recent church fire, in June 2005, burned down Sacred Heart in Weymouth Landing, but it has been replaced, as churches typically are. This is a Catholic parish. While Weymouth now has five

Catholic parishes, Catholic services were not held in town until the middle of the 1800s, when the first priests arrived, Fathers Roddan and Lynch. The first Catholic parish was St. Francis Xavier, and it included the whole town of Weymouth. The growth in the next one hundred years or so was rapid.

Those early masses were held in private homes, but within a few months services were held in Tirrell's Hall at Weymouth Landing. The first Catholic church was, like two of today's parishes, located on Washington Street, the geographic center of town at Middle Street, where the town hall was also located. Father Roche was in charge of this parish, but it was a mission (sub-parish) of the Abington Parish. The first Weymouth pastor (1866–69) was Father Timothy Hannigan, who was followed by Reverend Hugh P. Smyth. This building also burned down in 1869, attributed to arson.

In what today would be viewed as controversial, Catholic mass was said in the old town house (the equivalent of today's town hall) for one year.

A second St. Francis Xavier Church was built in 1871 in South Weymouth. The present building on Pleasant Street dates from 1959 and is the third St. Francis.

Immaculate Conception began in a shoe factory near Jackson Square the following year. The flourishing shoemaking industry and the Weymouth Iron Works brought workers to East Weymouth, many of them Catholics. There were too many for existing buildings, and Reverend Hugh Smyth, who was in charge of churches in Weymouth and the South Shore, decided against rebuilding at Middle and Washington Streets.

Randall's Hall, where the first services were held in East Weymouth, was located in the rear of Canterbury's shop, but the cornerstone for a new church was laid the following year. A parish house was also built for the pastor, Father Millerick, who succeeded Father Hugh Smyth. The men of the parish did much of the work.

Father Smyth had also directed the building of a church at Weymouth Landing to be called Sacred Heart. There had been an influx of Catholics, mostly Irish, to the area around Weymouth Landing. In earlier decades, they had traveled to mass in South Boston and later West Quincy. Mass was also celebrated from time to time in homes of the area.

Father Smyth built eight churches on the South Shore and bought the old Wales Hotel on Commercial Street, as well as an inn called the

Half Way House, which would eventually become the rectory for the new church. He began Sacred Heart Parish in 1871, and the hotel was used for services until the church was completed in 1882.

The North Weymouth parish already had a wooden building for one hundred people located on Lovell Street behind today's church, built by Father Smyth in 1880. However, it was too small. People often had to stand outside listening through the windows as mass was said. This building caught fire from the furnace and burned to the ground on Palm Sunday 1914.

After the chapel burned, St. Jerome's parishioners attended the Immaculate Conception Church until the opening of the new church in 1915. In 1928, St. Jerome's became a separate parish. A rectory, built in 1935, was later moved down Neck Street, where it now serves as condos. The present church was built in 1964.

PART II

Industry and Transportation

Early Industries

The early settlers brought little with them from England, so they had to learn to produce their own food, furniture, buildings and wagons.

Settlers had to earn their living with the things they found waiting for them, and they had to get together with their neighbors to protect themselves and their families and figure out rules by which to live. There was no choice. They had to raise food or die, build houses or freeze. So until they could buy things from people in other lands, they made use of what they had, learned new skills and became quite good at all this.

The early settlers passed on to their children the efficiency and ingenuity that they had acquired, and these became characteristics of early New England settlements. They expected to work hard, long hours every day but the Sabbath.

Those qualities were carried over into the first industries, many of which were homegrown. It's not surprising that the first ones made use of natural resources rather than any specialized skills. One of the first ways of making a living began long before the settlers got here. In the summer, fishing was carried on in the rivers, along the shore and in weirs (or fishnets) by the American Indians who came to the area, especially North Weymouth.

Naturally, the settlers learned to catch the abundant fish and shellfish. In the early 1700s, the Fish Company was formed by a group of the men in Weymouth to operate a fishing trade on the Fore River by Hunt's Hill. In fact Sea Street was at first called Fish Street.

We know from early accounts that settlers were also catching the fish that Weymouth became famous for—herrings, or alewives. We know from reading reports from early town meetings that control of the herring brook was discussed as far back as 1648 and was, in fact, a regular topic of discussion.

The early settlers also farmed. The prime farming area was located in the north part of Weymouth, where most of the fertile soil lay. Farming was something some settlers knew from their time in England, while others learned it and then passed the knowledge and experience on to their children. Their chief crops were grains—especially corn and wheat. For the most part these were not pick-and-eat products. The wheat and the kind of corn they grew had to be ground in order to be used as flour in bread and other products. That meant that they had to build gristmills to grind the grain, and once again they used the things nature had given them.

The rivers—Fore and Back—had rapid running water, and that's where settlers built gristmills. They took advantage of the tides that flowed in and out of Mill Cove. Mill Cove is upriver from where the energy plant now stands on Fore River and just before where the section called "Idelwell" is now.

When the settlers got the mill to work as intended and provide them with edible food, it boosted their confidence—they had proved to themselves that they could really coax nature to do what they wanted. If mills would grind grain, then why not use flowing water for other things? So they tried it. William Waltham was the name of the man who built a sawmill and gristmill on Whitman's Pond near the location on Route 53 at which you can see the pond on both sides. At one time, falling water ran through there, allowing his mill to run.

A sawmill was perfect from the settlers' perspective because they had so many trees around them—too many, in fact, because they wanted to build houses and barns, and they needed both the space the trees were taking and the wood they would provide. With lumber from the sawmill, they could not only build their houses but also make furniture and useful things like plows, wagons and boats.

At first they just cut down trees, removed the bark and made boards, which they could fasten together with pegs (or nails if they were lucky enough to have brought some). The lumber business was an important one in Weymouth for hundreds of years, but it changed. After many of the trees had been cut down, it dawned on the settlers that they should decrease the number of trees felled, and they even passed laws that ordered as much. Although the town stayed in the lumber business, now the timber came to Weymouth from other places, and our forefathers milled it and got it ready to use.

Weymouth Landing had wharves that had been built at the mouth of Smelt Brook. Those were used to unload lumber shipped from Maine. Lumber companies existed at Weymouth Landing into the latter part of the twentieth century. They took the timber from the north woods and milled it so that it became usable wood. Then they transported it—first using horses and wagons and later trains and trucks—to settlements mostly to the south. Rhines Lumber was the final survivor of these companies. The last of these lumber companies stood on Commercial Street along the river not far from where the Old Colony Railroad tracks now pass below.

Shipbuilding was another early industry. Weymouth Landing had small yards, and there were shipyards in other parts of town, too, one being Keene at Hunt's Hill in North Weymouth. But Weymouth Landing had so many of the town's businesses that the first two banks in town were established there.

Another industrial resource was stone. The town was known especially for its seam-faced granite, which was quarried near Route 53 at the Hingham border. The igneous rock is hard and wears down slowly—perfect for public buildings meant to last.

Some notable public buildings are the Fogg Building (often called the Opera House) in Columbian Square, as well as the Fogg Library, which stands across the street from it. Those were built late in the 1800s, but granite continues to be used in town, as the Tufts Library from the 1960s will attest. More recently, granite has been used to face the underpasses of the Old Colony railroad at Weymouth Heights.

Agricultural pursuits were mainstays up until about the year 1800. By that time, the trades had taken over as the major way of making a living in Weymouth. That changeover would become almost total by the time that century had ended.

On Weymouth Neck, that transformation was easy to see. In 1872, the world's largest producer of phosphates for farming was built there—the Bradley Fertilizer Company. The company grew quickly. Farmers in the

The Fogg Building or "Opera House."

eastern and southern parts of the United States needed his products, and later, there was demand from all over the world, and he was employing hundreds of Weymouth workers in a complex of buildings. In the late 1800s, the company owned a large tugboat, *Peter B. Bradley*, that was nearly eighty feet long.

MORE INDUSTRIES

Weymouth residents of a certain age will recall the Edgar Edison Station built in 1925 to provide electric power to the area to Boston's south. The plant presented a great hulking presence as it loomed on the Weymouth shore of the Fore River across from the shipyard in Quincy. The station was quite a formidable welcome to the town of Weymouth.

The Edgar Edison Station was built in the art deco style, and its massive pile projected just what it was built for—power. When it was built, the Fore River Basin abandoned all appearances of being a serene stream. The stone and steel industries were now the hallmarks as one passed over the bridge on Route 3A. In fact, seen at night in a fog with

The Weymouth Iron Company.

greenish light around it, Edgar may well have looked like the castle of Jack's giant to a young child.

Imposing and indestructible as it seemed, it was, however, fated to last only until 1977; it became outdated and environmentally hazardous. The structure had been declared a national engineering landmark as the location of many technological advances, but it has since been replaced by no less an imposing structure, one that should be more environmentally friendly: the Fore River Station, with buildings and facilities on both sides of Route 3A along the Weymouth side of the river.

An industry that appeared in the mid-1800s made its mark on East Weymouth but is not well remembered. It flared like a Fourth of July sparkler and then fizzled and flamed out. This was the making of iron and steel products by the Weymouth Iron Company. Iron ore had been discovered early on in the bottom of the town's ponds.

Weymouth Iron quickly transformed East Weymouth around Jackson Square from rural to commercial and industrial—the company was, in reality, a small empire. The company had most of the facilities located on its own property to sustain it. This included more than thirty structures that ran from the river on Wharf Street and up Water Street to Iron Hill. From its establishment in 1837 until it closed in 1885, Weymouth Iron employed hundreds of workers. Among the properties and items it owned were a water wheel for power, dams, canals, a complete rolling mill, factories, a barrel shop and its own wharves.

The main thing the company made was nails. Adding to its self-sufficiency were a shop for making barrels and kegs to contain the nails and a carpenter's shop to make things such as wharves and buildings.

The water wheel was located near Iron Hill Street and required such quantities of water that it had to be shut down when it hadn't rained for some time. But the biggest building on the site held a 150-horsepower engine with bright brass work that stood upright. Near it and facing the yard were furnaces and the nail machine, which spit out nails and spikes like a machine gun. Then there were triphammers, squeezers and shears, all of which cut the nails and spikes into various sizes and shapes.

Then there were the piles of raw materials—iron ore, of course, plus pig iron, coal, flint and quartz. These materials all had to be shoveled into the furnaces to make iron and steel. Shirtless men sweated before the open doors of these furnaces, mixing the molten iron.

This hot, softened iron was then removed with long tongs and placed on rollers, where it was shaped and sized. It could be flattened out or cut into rods perhaps ten feet in length and at several different thicknesses. This depended on the nails and spikes that were needed.

People living in East Weymouth who wanted to sleep late must have been out of luck—when fires were started in the furnaces, they began to roar into the still-dark sky in the wee hours, sending a glow of red and plumes of flame skyward before the clock struck three o'clock.

The excess slag from these iron-making furnaces was dumped in the area downhill from Jackson Square, near the parking area uphill from the restaurant that stands there now. The mill had machines that cut iron into large nails and spikes, but it also made anchors, chains and other iron products.

All this industry meant an increase in the population of East Weymouth as people moved there to be near these jobs. The company owned twelve to fifteen tenements located right on its property, and a boardinghouse as well, but it didn't have enough housing for all its workers, so there was a golden opportunity for an entrepreneur. Cyrus Washburn saw the sparkle of gold and bought up neighborhoods of cheap housing made out of materials from houses in Boston that had been torn down. These were located on streets near Whitman's Pond, and Washburn did very nicely with his rentals and sales.

The iron company owned two wharves, as well as all those buildings. Both were located on the Back River, but one was near the company on Wharf Street while the other, on deeper water, was on Weymouth Neck near the present Back River Street, nearer the mouth of the river. This one handled coal from Sydney, Nova Scotia. Iron company workers off-loaded it onto wagons, and horses pulled them to Jackson Square. Some of the vessels on Back River were of an impressive size. People who live in North Weymouth today who like to watch the oceangoing tankers would have liked to stand and watch ships like the *General Lovell* plying the waters through Hull Gut to dock on the Back River. This huge, sixty-ton ship would then carry nails to Boston and bring back scrap iron.

Still, Weymouth wasn't destined to be an iron or steel town for long. Competition from elsewhere was too great. Mills in Pennsylvania had an advantage by being closer to the coal mines and iron ore range, so they outdid Weymouth financially.

Two can play at that game, and the owner of the next Weymouth factory was an ace at self-promotion. E.S. Hunt knew that you had to be creative and competitive, and he was both. His factory at the corner of Broad and King Streets produced fireworks and other nontraditional products.

Hunt was no newcomer to Weymouth. His family had lived there for years. His favored profession was that of scientist and inventor, but for many years he was perhaps best known for his production of fireworks. These weren't the kind that people carry around in a bag and toss. These were the kind that cities and towns pay to have set off in big displays. He made rockets and set pieces, as well as a specialty that he called "Dragon Wheels."

He had several inventions, including one for rescuing sailors from sinking ships, but the one that paid off for him was a new process for making ladies' fans. With his method you could both fold the fan and glue it to the stick all in one step—which was cheaper. He could also put gold leaf on the wooden sticks of the fans—very fancy. That's what the fans were, though. They were for fancy ladies—brides or society women who liked to carry them when the air was still or hot. Many of them were made of silk or satin and trimmed with gold sequins. He did pretty well selling them, especially right after the Civil War, but his best years of "fandom" lay ahead.

The fans made in Paris had the most cachet, but by 1870 you couldn't get them. France had gone to war with Prussia, and it didn't go well, so for a few years Hunt went into rapid production and cornered the market. Between waving fans and bursting fireworks, he did very well.

If you'd like to examine those fans, you can. They have a display at the museum on the bottom floor of Tufts Library, which is open Monday evenings. You can also see the Indian dugout canoe, a display about the ship *Edward Everett* and one about Weymouth's primary industry of the past—shoemaking.

SHOEMAKING

Lumber, stone, farming, fishing, shipbuilding, fans, fireworks, fertilizer, a woolen factory—these were all part of Weymouth's past. However, those industries are more or less extinct in this town now. That's also true of the industry that employed more Weymouth workers than any other at any time—the shoemaking industry. When it was at its high point, three out of four town workers were employed in some aspect of the leather industry. At that point, the town was nationally known as a place that manufactured boots and shoes of the highest quality.

Like all industries, shoemaking began on a small, homemade scale. In fact, the first men who made shoes were itinerant cobblers who went from home to home making or repairing shoes or boots. It was kind of like getting a repairman of any kind to come to your house today—you had to make an appointment.

There was a major difference, though. He would bring his tools and his clothes, and he would live with the family until the work was done. Usually the household would turn over a corner of the kitchen for his workshop. The main piece of equipment was a shoemaker's bench, which was really a combination bench and toolbox with drawers that could be hauled on a cart.

The shoemaker would measure everyone's foot and then make a mold called a "last" from a piece of wood. The last would be shaped like the person's foot. Only one last was made because until 1785 the left and right shoes would be the same. The shoemaker would then write the name on the last until he got around to making the shoes.

A visit from a shoemaker was something families looked forward to because these men were walking rumor mills. They brought news and gossip since they traveled all over town and picked up juicy tidbits at each stop. Many cobblers liked the job because of this very aspect.

An early shoemaker.

They were chatty, and they brought a change from everyday life. Some had sidelines, too—they might bring along a pair of pliers and pull teeth.

Cobblers also came with a cost since there were just a few of them for hire in the early days, and they could charge what the traffic would allow.

As with most people who were being overcharged, Weymouth farmers tried to save money by making and wearing durable and stretchable Indian-style moccasins, or else they watched closely while the cobbler worked and then tried it for themselves. You can see for

"Ten-footers" served as shoemaking shops.

yourself the display on shoemaking and its techniques at the Tufts Library on Broad Street.

If you were a young man in Weymouth at that time, it might seem more interesting to make shoes than to farm, for example, and a lot of young men learned the trade. A side benefit was the money you could save on footwear for your family.

The day of the traveling cobbler was ending, and that of the "ten-footer" had begun. These were workshops, ten feet by ten feet in size, built by a worker in his backyard for shoemaking. Some of them are still around. The Weymouth Historical Society has one located behind the Holbrook House on Park Avenue.

The ten-footers had one large window for light, with a bench in front of it. They needed a tub of water for soaking the leather and also a "lasting jack," a vertical shaft of cast iron with a kind of knob on top. It stood on the floor, and the shoemaker did his work on top of it.

Shoes or boots made at the ten-footers were made to order. They called it "bespoke" work—work that the customer had ordered ahead of time, and the shoemaker knew he would be paid for his work and his leather. It wasn't like a shoe store where you had to have many types and sizes on hand in the hope that someone would buy them. He didn't have to tie up his capital or take the risk that he would not see remuneration on some of his work.

It was cheaper for the customer if he provided his own leather. That way the shoemaker didn't have to buy a lot of leather that he might not use.

Adam Dagys built the first factory for making shoes in 1780 in Lynn. We think of factories as a place where workers arrive and depart together or in shifts, punching time clocks. But in this case, much of the work was done at home and brought to the factory to be assembled with other work.

That was also how it worked in the first Weymouth factory, built by James Tirrell in 1808. Tirrell's factory was located on Front Street very near the spot where the Front Street overpass crosses Route 3 today. Employees did some of the work on Front Street, but much of it was done by individual shoemakers at home in their ten-footers. They even had wives or children do some of the pieces. Finally, all the pieces were assembled in the factory.

The factory also sold the shoes. Once or twice per week, shoes were put in the saddlebags of horses and taken to Boston. In some cases they were then packed in barrels and shipped to outlying places like New Orleans or other points south. New Orleans is worth mentioning because Tirrell had business associates in New Orleans, where he had formerly sold shoes and boots to the early planters. Those barrels were then used to ship molasses back to Boston, where it was used as a sweetener or to make rum. It was also used with baked beans, for which Boston would become famous. The "Yankee Trader" Tirrell made profits coming and going.

When Weymouth shoes were sold elsewhere—where there were no shoe factories—they had quite a markup. By 1790, a pair of men's shoes cost three dollars in Massachusetts, where there were many shoemakers. But in the rural outpost of California, the same shoes would cost you eleven dollars.

The Stetson Shoe Company.

Tirrell's shoes were rather plain, and his boots were serviceable, as were others of that time. But progress lay ahead. In the mid-1800s, machinery to make shoes was invented, and after the Civil War nearly all the work was done in factories. The shoes began to have some style.

The invention of the sewing machine in 1846 by Elias Howe certainly helped. It was first used for shoes by Elias Beals, who owned a shoe factory on Sea Street right across from where the North Weymouth Post Office now stands.

Other machines followed. Lyman Blake invented a machine in 1858 that sewed soles to uppers, and sixteen years later a welt-stitcher, invented by Charles Goodyear Jr., brought high-quality welt shoes made by machines.

Then in 1882 an immigrant shoe factory worker named Ernest Matzeliger, son of a Dutch engineer and a native black woman from Surinam, invented the shoe-lasting machine, which allowed factories to make shoes very quickly and therefore more cheaply. He didn't get rich or famous, though. His patents were bought by the new United Shoe Machinery Company, and it did so well that shoe prices in the United States were cut in half, while workers' wages doubled and working conditions improved for what were then millions of shoemaking workers.

United Shoe wouldn't sell its machines, though; it would only lease them. Then, like some of today's software companies, those who leased were given the chance to upgrade when improved machines came along. Even then you didn't own the machine; you just got the new parts.

Besides, the machines came with a counter, and those who leased were also charged according to the number of times they used the machines. That meant that United got royalties on each pair of shoes made with its machines. This monopoly paid for the first skyscraper in Boston (which still stands on High Street).

Stetson Shoe began in 1885. Its products would become known nationwide. Indeed, Weymouth shoes and boots in general were known for their quality across the land. If something was "Weymouth Grade," you knew it was top of the line. Stetson lasted until 1973, when it became the last Weymouth shoe factory to close its doors. But the building was saved. Today it functions as "Stetson Place," and it has many of the features of a nineteenth-century building, including exposed beams and brick on the interior.

Beautifully restored, it houses clinics and other medical facilities and accommodates a high count of daily traffic, probably more than it ever did in its life as a shoe factory. There have been many Weymouth shoe factories over time. Another example, the John S. Fogg Boot Factory building, still stands at the corner of Union Street in Columbia Square, now converted to other uses. But the shoe industry meant more than the major factories. There were also small-scale shoemakers in all parts of town, and there were other shops that were adjuncts to the shoe industry making things like laces, heels and tacks. There were tanneries, too.

However, at the peak of the shoemaking trade, Weymouth had become largely a one-industry town. Fortunately, that industry died out slowly and over many years. That gave the town a chance to bring in other things that could take its place.

The Stetson Place medical offices.

The shoemaking industry and others defined Weymouth as a working-class town, and it still is mostly that. Much of the housing stock from that era was built by people in that industry and are not fancy.

Weymouth does not have many mansions nor does it have notable slum areas. Homes with water or ocean views are the highest priced, but in all, the town remains dependably working class. In the year 2009, it listed 131 homes valued in excess of $1 million and 237 for less than $200,000.

THE HERRING ARE COMING! THE HERRING ARE COMING!

Herring are actually alewives, but by any name, they run through East Weymouth each spring, raising the traditional cry "The herring are here! The herring are here!" The herring run is an annual Weymouth event, and it's also a tradition for parents to take their children to watch the transit and explain what's happening.

These herring (or alewives) caught the attention of our earliest settlers. Weymouth had been run by a gathering of its voters (town meeting) since 1624. Minutes were kept starting in 1641, and the "herring brogue" (the word for "brook" in the English of Chaucer) appears in the records for 1648. The rarity of herring brooks caused William Wood to comment in his *New England's Prospect*: "The outmost plantation…is called Wichaguscusset, an Indian name (Weymouth)…Here the inhabitants have good stores of fish of all sorts…Here is likewise an Alewife river." So what are alewives and why do they "run"?

These herring live in coastal waters of the Atlantic Ocean. At the time of year when the water in the ponds becomes warmer than that in the ocean—usually fifty-five to sixty degrees Fahrenheit—the alewives swim upriver to the ponds to spawn or lay their eggs. The females lay thousands of eggs, which sink to the bottom of the ponds and pools and attach to the rocks and pebbles in the mud at the bottom. The adult fish then return to the sea.

The new fish hatch and spend the summer in waters like Whitman's Pond, and in the fall the young fish—two to four inches long—move down the streams to the sea. By the time spring comes around again, these fish are now ten to twelve inches long and fully grown. The cycle is repeated.

In his book *The Outermost House*, author Henry Beston muses more lyrically:

> *Somewhere in the depths of the ocean each Weymouth-born fish remembers Whitman's Pond, and comes to it through the directionless leagues of the sea. What stirs in each cold brain? What call quivers, as the new sun strikes down the river of ocean? How do the creatures find their way? Whatever the reason, the herring are "in" at Weymouth, breasting the brook's overflow to the ancestral pond.*

So in the spring we see the adults swimming upstream and back, often passing other alewives. In the summer the young fish swim out to the Back River up until October. Some years an estimated 200,000 have "remembered Whitman's Pond" and made it upstream.

This anadromous habit, as it is called, impressed the early settlers on our coasts. In the words of an eyewitness, "Experience hath taught them at New Plymouth that in April there is a fish much like a herring that comes up into the small brooks to spawn, and when the water is not knee deep they will presse up through your hands, yea, thow you beat at them with cudgels, and in such abundance as is incredible." We no longer have to beat at their masses with cudgels, but still they come.

The alewife is much more heavily built than the herring (or sea herring), the front part of its body appearing to have a beer gut. An "alewife" was a woman who brewed and sold beer. These human alewives must have consumed their product often, since it was their large bellies that made fishermen think of them when they saw the wide-bellied fish. The alewife, like the herring, is grayish green above, darkest on the back and paler and silvery on sides and belly.

The adults, when entering streams to spawn, make the change from salt water to fresh within a short time without damage; this is equally true of the spent fish on their return to the estuaries. Like the herring, the alewife eats mostly the tiny plankton but may eat small fish. They don't eat while they are running upstream to spawn, but once they return to brackish waters like the Back River, it's the "Alewife Mardi Gras" and they feed voraciously to make up for all their fasting. In the ocean, they gather in large schools and may be found in waters as far north as the St. Lawrence River in Canada and as far south as North Carolina.

Alewives are quite edible fish and are sold both fresh and salted. They can be used as bait for the fish of George's and Stellwagon Banks around Massachusetts Bay, and back in the 1920s their scales were used to make artificial pearls. Most of them are caught in or near river mouths, and many are taken by birds or in fish traps. They have always had to overcome difficulties to return to Whitman's Pond. In the first place, it's not easy to swim upstream, and boulders, strong currents, tree branches and other obstacles make it even harder. Weymouth residents have felt responsible for these fish and wanted them to continue their yearly voyages, so they took extraordinary steps to make Weymouth "alewife friendly."

On March 8, 1724, a committee was chosen at the town meeting "to treat with the mill owners on the river, by Bates; to make a convenient passage for fish into Whitman's Pond, to pay out over five pounds." From then on, the run occupies considerable space in the town records. Officers were selected regularly to protect the fish and to supervise the small alewife fishery, the proceeds of which went to the town. The concrete run that we have now was built in the 1940s by the Department of Marine Fisheries. It has fish ladders or steps, which make the uphill climb easier for the fish. Each year, though, repairs to the passageway are needed, and every year in early April, volunteers are called for a cleanup of the herring run. In a few hours on the first Saturday of April, they remove truckloads of debris.

In recent years, other changes have been made to alleviate flooding conditions, and then recently the flood control gate had to be repaired so that the fish could get by. At present, the run begins at Whitman's Pond and flows through and under the Iron Hill area, passing under Commercial Square. It flows past the town incinerator, into Back River and out to sea. Town meetings also made rules to control fishing so that there would *be* herring to come back year after year. You could only take so many, and you had to pay to fish at the brook. At one time, 100,000 herring were taken in one day. This became hard to manage. The town didn't want to be in the fish warden business, so in 1845 it sold the rights to the herring to the Weymouth Iron Company, which had headquarters located near Jackson Square. In the 1860s, citizens of Weymouth paid one dollar for four hundred fish. Out-of-towners had to pay double. Weymouth is still trying to control fishing, and the ratio for out-of-towners is the same, though the cost for Weymouthites has increased fivefold. Residents and nonresidents can purchase permits that allow them to bring in a dozen fish per week. Once you have your permit, you are entitled to bring in fish during the designated "dipping" times, you may only dip at the Middle Pool at the corner of Commercial and Water Streets in Commercial Square and you're expected to stop when you have twelve.

Some people, mostly from outside of Weymouth, are poachers. They've heard about the herring run, and they come to Weymouth to help themselves. But they don't help the herring run survive. Many of the age-old herring runs in Massachusetts have been closed so that the number of fish could build back again. Weymouth's run is one of the oldest, and it's a survivor because the people of Weymouth have protected it—like Great Esker, the estuary in Back River and the land at Weymouth Neck.

If the run survives, the children of Weymouth will probably bring their children to watch the alewives. It's something uncommon and it fascinates people. I have a theory that people like to root for the underdog, and these fish are certainly that. In their silvery splashing we can see the struggle for procreation—it's a heroic struggle to survive against tough obstacles by small, nearly helpless creatures, and they thrive in spite of the odds against them. Survival against the odds began at Wessagusset settlement long ago and has become another Weymouth tradition.

Transportation

Weymouth grew faster than many towns because when settlers felt the need to spread out from their coastal roots, they already had a road system for travel. These weren't highways, of course, or even paved roads. What they had was a network of Indian trails they could follow wherever they wanted to go.

Because of their coastal location and their proximity to places frequented by the Indians, an inordinate number of these trails ran though Weymouth, and the colonists followed them as they moved from North Weymouth to what would become population centers. In later times, the trails became roads that would help them trade with other places, just as the Indians had.

The Indians, you see, had been blazing trails for hundreds of years across Weymouth during their hunting, fishing and trading expeditions, and those trails were destined to become major roads as the town developed. Our ancestors had developed the Yankee trait of making good use of whatever was provided for them. It would be no different when it came to building roads where one had already been started.

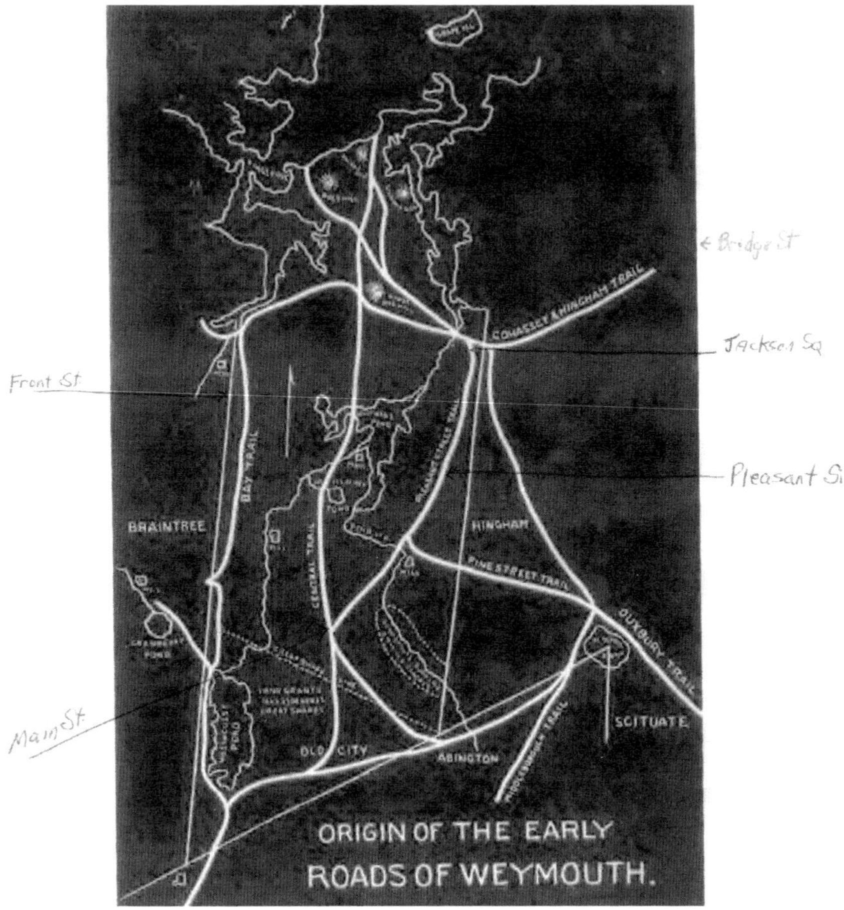

Trails that became roads.

At first, the roads were only paths, but they were well marked and easy to follow. Their courses made good sense to the Indians, and at first they made sense to the settlers, too. The native people had followed the contours of the land, and when they came to a water obstacle or a hill, they just went around it. Rivers and ponds were good for travel, as well as for laying fishing nets and finding waterfowl to hunt, so it's not surprising that many trails went from one pond to another and along the rivers to the ocean. Those were the areas in which the Indians spent time.

When settlers went from place to place, they just followed those trails. They built homes, stores and churches on or near those trails. When they made better roads, it was actually the Indian trails that they improved. Most of them are heavily used even today.

The Coastal Trail is known today as Commercial Street; it starts at Weymouth Landing and runs along the river to Weymouth Heights and King Oak Hill. After climbing the side of the hill, it veers left past Legion Field and winds into Jackson Square before dipping down the rise into Commercial Square. Another trail, the Plymouth and Duxbury Trail, starts in East Weymouth.

When the Coastal Trail ran into the side of King Oak Hill, it began another branch to the left that became North Street and ran between the hills at the cemetery and on to the coast via Neck and Sea Streets. These routes are exactly where the Indians' Coastal Trail ran. It isn't surprising that many of the oldest houses in Weymouth stand along these trails that became streets. Even if the houses don't date back to the 1600s, they probably once stood among houses that did.

A trail that ran north–south was the Bay Trail. This, too, began at Weymouth Landing. It ran up today's Front Street to Summer Street. Then it made a little zigzag onto West, Columbia and Forest Streets. It ran the length of today's Forest to Randolph Street and Great Pond. From there it continued south through other towns into Rhode Island, all the way to Narragansett Bay, where there were many American Indians with whom to trade.

Central Trail ran along today's Middle Street from Legion Field to where Stetson Place now stands on Main Street; Pleasant Street Trail began at Jackson Square and ran to Independence Square, and Pine Street Trail ran from today's Pleasant Street and joined the Duxbury Trail near Accord Pond.

In 1723, when the south precinct was formed, the church was placed near a trail that ran to Independence Square and down Union Street to Rockland. From there, the streets around Columbian Square radiated out in several directions from the meetinghouse and connected with one another.

So the main roads of Weymouth derived from Indian trails. Some connected with roads to other places. To get to Boston during the first 150 years you took a small boat called a packet or you used a horse or wagon on poor, rutted roads. As the roads improved, stagecoaches appeared on three routes through Weymouth.

Queen Anne's Turnpike was built in 1805 and ran between Weymouth and Braintree. In 1852, it became known as Washington Street, a name that remains. The New Bedford Turnpike became Main Street or Route 18, and in 1912, a toll road was built across North Weymouth between

An old-fashioned trolley on Sea Street.

Quincy and Hingham, with toll bridges stretching across the Fore and Back Rivers. In 1862, it became a public highway known as Route 3A. Tollbooths also stood for a time in Braintree at Weymouth Landing and at the Hingham end of Route 53.

So the trails turned into roads, and people used them to move to other parts of town. Unlike most places with populations of about fifty-five thousand people, Weymouth has no center. It has places called "villages." The main ones are Weymouth Landing, Jackson Square, Columbian Square and Bicknell Square. There are also smaller ones like Lovell's Corner, Weymouth Heights Independence Square and Commercial Square.

At first the streets had no names. In 1837, when the town picked a committee to name streets and note where they were, they used people's names or landmarks. For example: "The street leading from the seashore, near Edward Blanchard's to North Street near James Thomas', shall be called Sea Street."…"The street leading from North Street, near the former residence of Samuel Humphrey, now deceased shall be called Neck Street [this street now crosses Bridge Street and extends to the sea]."…"The turnpike leading from Ferry Point Bridge to Back River Bridge shall be called Bridge Street."

After the roads came the railroads. Many people opposed them, just as the recent incarnation met opposition. A line from Braintree crossed South Weymouth to Abington in 1845. It was the first to be called the

Weymouth Landing from East Braintree.

"Old Colony Railroad" but not the last. An enterprising person ran an express stagecoach like a taxi from Weymouth Landing to the Braintree Depot so Weymouth citizens could have train service.

In 1849, a line was built through Weymouth Landing, North Weymouth and East Weymouth. Though it ran essentially over the route of today's Old Colony, it was called the South Shore Railroad. The railroads helped to develop the town. Wherever the lines ran, people moved in and businesses opened, a foreshadowing of today's "smart growth."

By the 1890s the town was ready for internal transit. The street railway already joined Weymouth to Boston. For many years, the vehicles were trolley cars, usually painted orange and running on a track down the center of a street. You could tell where they would stop by an orange band painted on a telegraph pole. The main trolley route ran along Broad Street from Weymouth Landing to East Weymouth. There was also a branch that ran along Middle, North, Neck and River Streets to North Weymouth and one from the Landing to South Weymouth using Front and Main Streets.

A Pleasant Street line connected East and South Weymouth, and a Union Street line ran to Rockland. If you put a nickel in the fare box, you could ride anywhere in Weymouth. You could also connect with lines in adjacent towns.

Little by little, the trolleys were phased out and buses took their place. These bus lines now run on numbered routes and schedules, usually starting or ending in Red Line T stations.

The major change in transportation in Weymouth and elsewhere came during the 1920s and 1930s, when the automobile came into popular use. That was the end of the trolleys, and cars brought more people and more housing developments to town—especially in the late 1940s after World War II had ended. By the end of that decade, Weymouth's population had reached nearly today's levels.

More cars meant more roads, and the most important one split Weymouth in half. Route 3 connected Boston with Cape Cod. It makes Weymouth easier to reach or leave, but it separates the south part of town from the rest as effectively as the second church did. Those who want to get to Boston without traffic can catch a commuter boat at Hingham or Quincy or board the Old Colony Railroad at East Weymouth or Weymouth Landing. It follows the route that was abandoned in 1959.

The early roads and the railroad helped the town's industries to grow. But more recent modes have taken most of the industry to other places and transformed Weymouthites into commuters.

The present time seems to be a "plateau" in the growth of transportation, but history only *appears* to have plateaus. Things are still happening even though change is less obvious.

PART III

Parts of Town

The Bradleys and Weymouth Neck

If William L. Bradley and his son Peter B. Bradley are remembered in Weymouth, it's usually for the fertilizer plant that was one of their many thriving businesses. And if the plant is remembered, it's probably for the materials that lodged themselves in the long-term memory of the area, requiring a cleanup many years later.

In Meriden, Connecticut, William Bradley is remembered and his contributions are memorialized. He could have traced his ancestors on both sides to the first settlers in the New Haven area. They came there as "planters" of the colony just after the time when Weymouth was incorporated as a town.

William started his business career as a clerk in a dry goods store in New Haven and followed that by becoming a traveling salesman. He was very successful and soon started something new. With his brother and a friend he began to manufacture clocks and metal wares, a business that became the Bradley & Hubbard Manufacturing Company, the largest industry of its kind in the world.

Now prosperous, William Bradley bought land in the small city of Meriden and built a fine house, which still stands. He gradually added to the land until he had two hundred acres. Part of the land was used for the annual Meriden Fair with a track on which horse races were run. (The house is now the clubhouse for the Meriden Golf Club, and upscale housing has been built on the acreage as arranged by the Bradleys.)

In 1861, William Bradley began the manufacture of chemical fertilizers in South Bay, a shoreline section of Boston, and the business grew so quickly that he built another, larger factory on Weymouth Neck. It eventually became the largest fertilizer plant in the world. The fertilizers were used all over the world, and so there was shipping to go with it. The location on the Back River was chosen partly for this reason.

In 1872, the business was incorporated under the name of the Bradley Fertilizer Company, and William Bradley set up branch offices in Rochester, Cleveland, Baltimore and Augusta, Georgia. He served as CEO and manager. He also operated huge phosphate mines in South Carolina and Florida and had other fertilizer plants in New Jersey, Ohio, Maryland and South Carolina. But the one in North Weymouth was the largest.

Just as it had been his habit in Connecticut, Bradley also acquired real estate, including Weymouth Neck, Fort Point and Great Hill, as well as one hundred acres in North Hingham. Unfortunately, he had worked so hard and kept the pressure on himself for so many years that his health suffered from it, and William Bradley retired to his Hingham estate, leaving his business, including the Weymouth plant, to his sons Peter B. and Robert S. Bradley. William died in Hingham at age sixty-eight.

Bradley's land, Fort Point and Great Hill.

Peter became interested in horses as a boy, but this passion grew during his Weymouth years. At the age of forty-three he was at the Chicago World's Fair of 1893 when he saw an exhibition of Arabian horses that had been brought to America as what can be considered a cultural exchange. Bradley was enthralled. When the horses were auctioned off, he bought at least a dozen and brought them home to what would become known as the "Hingham Stock Farm." He would eventually have stalls for fifty mares and foals, as well as a racetrack.

Someone else was at that World's Fair, too. A young cartoonist for the *Chicago Herald* named Homer Davenport was captivated by the beauty of the Arabian horses. A few years later, he learned that Bradley had brought many of these Arabians to Hingham. He went to see him and bought one of them. More importantly, though, the two established a business relationship.

Davenport had an important connection, too. Because of his fame as a political cartoonist, he was known to politicians, including President Theodore Roosevelt. In those days, the Ottoman Empire, which controlled the horse-breeding countries of the Middle East, had a policy against exporting mares. You could buy the stallions but not the mares. Roosevelt intervened with the sultan on Davenport's behalf and got the policy changed. More horses came across the ocean to live on the land by the Back River.

Some people's achievements are absorbed into the fabric of progress until they are no longer identified with the contributions they have made. This happened to Peter Bradley in the subculture of horse breeding, which was his great love. However, the Bradleys were also great industrialists, and the byproducts of their fertilizer plant, though buried in the past, have surfaced again in our own generation.

Since the Civil War, Bradley Fertilizer made its product on Weymouth Neck and buried byproducts there as well. Not only whalebone, but also arsenic and lead were later found there. No one thought about those things in those days.

In 1899, the plant burned down, but the company was followed by the American Agricultural Chemical Company. Raw materials used in the production of fertilizer were stored there, and byproducts were disposed of in a landfill on the property. Two other fires in 1913 and 1946 would also have released harmful chemicals.

In 1966, Conoco acquired the land and sold it to a developer who had a grand plan to build condominiums and much more—even a

The Bradley fertilizer factory and docks.

heliport. However, the corporation that planned the development went bankrupt. Another developer bought part of the land for condos, and the state used the rest to create Webb Memorial State Park. The first set of condominiums was called Weymouthport. It was built on a small portion of the former Bradley Fertilizer land. There is also a marina at Tern Harbor and another set of condominium called East Bay just north of Weymouthport.

Sixteen acres of the land belong to Webb Memorial State Park and occupy the peninsula that has the Fore River on one side and the Back River on the other. You can stand on Sansone Point and watch them flow together. Beginning in April 1955, the U.S. military operated a Nike missile site on the hilly part of the parkland in conjunction with Fort Duvall in Hull. In the ten years between 1964 and 1974, the Army National Guard operated the site. Then in 1977, the state Department of Environmental Management (DEM) made "Webb State" a waterfront park. Three years later, it capped the site, part of which had been used as a landfill.

During the 1980s and '90s, investigations of the landfill area done by the state, EPA and private parties have found arsenic, lead and other contaminants in the soil. The condominiums at Weymouthport received an environmental "Notice of Responsibility." This meant that Weymouthport (and its residents) were the current owners and had to clean up the contamination within five years. It appeared that the condo dwellers would be liable for millions of dollars in cleanup costs.

However, the trustees hired Environmental Partners Group (EPG) to deal with the problem and also hired an environmental lawyer. He sent letters to all the previous owners. In less than a month they had a response from ConocoPhillips. Although Conoco had owned the property, it had not operated there, but the company nonetheless agreed to take care of the cleanup and even repay the state more than $500,000 for the costs that had already been incurred.

As it turned out, the dangers were not as great as some feared. Lead and arsenic become dangerous when they are airborne and can be inhaled. These ones were in the ground and could be buried. The "hot spots" could be placed within a common area, covered with textile and capped with three feet of new soil. Only a small amount of soil had to be removed from the site; most was shifted around, with new landscaping designed around the consolidation.

The digging also proved an opportunity to do some new landscaping. Some trees that blocked water views were replaced with ones that won't grow as full or tall, a new tennis court replaced two older ones, picnic areas were revamped and the Webb Memorial State Park that resulted from all the work is a gem of greenery along the ocean side with many walking trails and high points that look out toward Boston and the Harbor Islands. Scores of people walk the trails daily.

Back River, Great Esker

Weymouth's coastline was formed during the glacial periods. The advance and retreat of these ice sheets left behind two rivers, some coastal islands, great hills called drumlins, narrow ridges called eskers and the tidal estuary of Weymouth Back River.

All of these gifts left behind for our use were bestowed stealthily, as if by some secret Santa who wished to show us that Weymouth was one of his favorite places. People's use of Fore River provides an exhibit of what industrialization can do to nature. It's a beehive of industry and commerce, a far cry from the "beautiful bay" described by early observers. We prized its power but not its beauty.

We also have the subtler gift of the Back River. It's a rare and precious treasure because it's a special place that provides the beginnings of life of many kinds and is one of the few tidal estuaries of its type on the Atlantic Coast that is also within view of a major city. The way we treat it will determine our endowment to future generations.

Parts of the Weymouth Back River shoreline are a gift from the people of Weymouth, as well as from the forces of nature. In addition to its natural phenomena, Back River bears marks of historical significance, too, as we shall see.

Weymouth Neck, where the two rivers meet, was stamped rather indelibly by the Bradleys, who owned the fertilizer plant there and left contamination, which was cleaned up. One can stand at Sansone Point in Webb State Park and watch the mixing of the waters of Weymouth's two rivers.

At one time there were docks at the present Weymouthport condominium complex and also near today's Back River Road. Across from that dock area, on the Hingham/Weymouth line, is the peninsula called Stodder's Neck. It was once a gravel pit but has been landscaped and made into a park with walking trails and a fine view from its central hill of much of the Back River. The park is a favorite spot for dogs and their owners.

In the summer of 2003, seven acres of land on the north side of Route 3A that had been purchased in 1987 were finally turned into Abigail Adams Park. This park has trails with markers depicting the life of the second first lady, ample parking and a pleasant serenity hidden downslope from the fast-paced Route 3A.

From the mid-1630s, when Hingham and Weymouth became towns, the people in both places wanted to cross Back River. A ferry took them across for many years after 1637. The bridge that now spans the river was repaired in 2008. This present-day bridge replaced the "London Bridge" drawbridge that stood there from 1812. It had also been a toll bridge until Elias Beals of North Weymouth convinced the state legislature to remove the tolls on both ends of Bridge Street (Route 3A).

London Bridge was not falling down; it just took a long time to open and close. The bridge stayed there until Governor Leverett Saltonstall issued an executive order on September 3, 1942, to have it replaced by a span-type bridge in the interest of national security. Executive Order

Abigail Adams Park, Route 3A.

Number 34 began by saying that nobody had any right to do what he was about to do. But he did it anyway.

Shortages of critical materials caused by World War II would not allow the bridge machinery to be repaired, and it would be cheaper and quicker to build a new bridge. The ammo must move, so the bridge must go. If you can't lower the river, raise a new bridge.

The governor went on to say that the state was acting in cooperation with the navy and that local governments had all agreed with the plan. So it wasn't as high-handed as the name "Executive Order" might suggest. All of this points to the efficiencies brought about by war and to the ability to cut through red tape rather quickly when we really want to cut through it. The bridge had to be at least seventy feet above the water. The U.S. government was paying for everything, including any damages that resulted. The bridge was completed in well under a year and opened in 1943.

So now that we've gone under the bridge—which has just been refurbished—let's take a look at the rest of the river. The mouth, as we know, is the confluence with Fore River. The sources are streams in Hingham and Weymouth, including the Mill River, which begins in Great Pond and flows through Whitman's (once called Fresh) Pond to Jackson Square.

It is now possible to walk along most of the banks of Weymouth Back River, and the town has announced plans to connect the underused

Abigail Adams Park with Great Esker Park, which ought to enhance both properties when it happens. But there was a time within the memory of many when the banks of the river were off limits to the general public.

In 1910, the U.S. government took, by eminent domain, the land that is now Great Esker Park on the Weymouth side of the river and the land that is now Bare Cove Park on the Hingham side. In Hingham, nearly seven hundred acres had been taken in 1903 and was used as an ammunition depot for the Atlantic Fleet. Then the Weymouth side of the river was taken as a buffer zone that would keep people and boats at bay.

By 1965, the government had no further use for the Weymouth side of the river. It offered to sell it back to Weymouth at a discount provided that the land was used as a park and that a report on its use was filed every two years. Since the time of the Wessagusset settlement, the town was governed by town meeting. In 1965, that meant that each precinct had representatives at the town meeting and that they made the final decisions.

The boards in the town government were expected to make recommendations, and every board in town recommended *against* buying the land. But many private citizens disagreed. They thought it was a great idea and lobbied their town meeting representatives to vote for it.

Democracy won. The town meeting voted to buy it for $112,500 on October 24, 1966, and the following spring a small additional fund was raised for some improvements to the area. As we look back, it appears that the citizens knew what they were talking about.

So what did we buy along the banks of the Back? When Thomas Jefferson purchased the Louisiana Territory on our behalf two hundred years ago, he sent out a surveying party headed by Meriwether Lewis and William Clark. He wanted to know what he'd bought. Lewis and Clark sent back reports, samples and maps.

In the same way, the town conducted a survey by geologists, botanists, archaeologists and others. We learned that the land runs for about 1.5 miles along the Back River. We already knew that the Herring Run goes through the area each spring. A wide salt marsh of about one hundred acres separates the water from the eskers. They found much more besides.

They found a great esker, for example, named such. Eskers are long, narrow ridges left behind by glaciers—huge layers of ice, miles wide and sometimes a mile or more thick. Scientists called this molded land left by glaciers "esker" from the Irish-Gaelic word *eiscir*, meaning "ridge." There aren't many eskers left in the country, and ours is exceptional. It runs most of the length of the park and rises as high as ninety feet above the river near the Puritan Road entrance. It's the highest esker in the region. The paved road that runs along the top of the esker was actually a patrol road used by the navy when the park was a buffer zone. The navy also took some of the esker near the shopping plaza (afterward called "Hobo Flats"), using the dirt to build runways at South Weymouth Naval Air Station.

The esker shielded the river from view on the Weymouth side. One writer has called it "the Great Wall of Weymouth." At the same time, the height of the patrol road allowed the men patrolling it to see for long distances. In fact, if you want to get the best views both *of* the esker and *from* the esker, early spring is the time to go before the trees get their leaves. You'll be amazed at what you can see from there.

The 237 acres include 90 acres of marshland. The marshlands took nature an incredible twenty thousand years to build. They act like sponges to absorb flood tides and also make the food that the marine life needs and can't get anywhere else. It's like a specialty store for small wildlife and the only one of its kind around.

The area teems with wildlife of all sizes, including breeding grounds for dozens of kinds of birds, fish and shellfish and unusual types of plant life, as well as many small animals. We know about the herring, but there is also an eel fishery. These eels hatch from eggs laid in the Sargasso Sea far south in the Atlantic. One of the smaller streams has a smelt-breeding spot, and there are clam beds as well. Besides the herring, smelt and eels, Back River has bass, mackerel, haddock, cod, bluefish, flounder and Atlantic salmon.

Great Esker is also great for its geological features—not only the esker, but also the kettleholes, small ponds formed by chunks of ice in the glacial era, located at spots like Sugar Plum Ridge, Hockley Gut and the Bathtub. At Reversing Falls there was once an early gristmill.

There is folklore like the tale of the ghost of Aunt Molly, the murdered daughter of Chief Hunan, the Dinosaur's Bedroom and the story about the Whale Island Club. There's also an archaeological site from nine thousand years ago at which artifacts of an old Indian camping ground have been found.

WEBB STATE AND GRAPE ISLAND

If you enter Webb Memorial State Park from the parking area you will see a number of gravel-coated paths, known collectively as the Robert Ambler Walkway.

Veer to the right toward the Back River, and you are likely to see small boats and an occasional ferry to Boston. The land across Back River and to the right from you is an area of Hingham known as Hewitt's Cove. On it they had a small airstrip, a polo field and stables for horses. In addition to his phosphate interests, Peter Bradley introduced the Arabian horse into America, and he kept them just across the river there.

During World War II, a naval shipyard occupied that area, and it is currently being developed into high-end housing along with shops and restaurants. Commuter boats run to Boston from Hewitt's Cove.

As you look north, the island you see just ahead is Grape Island, a part of Weymouth that has an interesting story. A monument just ahead explains what happened.

Hewitt's Cove development.

Grape Island from Webb State Park.

On May 21, 1775, three small British ships anchored just below Great Hill in the Fore River, and British soldiers got into longboats. The story was told in a letter by Abigail Adams. Here's what she wrote:

> *It was difficult to tell their design, some supposed they were coming to Germantown, others to Weymouth.*
>
> *The alarm flew like lightning and men from all parts came flocking down till 2000 were collected—but it seems their expedition was to Grape Island for Leavitt's hay.*
>
> *Our people landed upon the island, and in an instant set fire to the hay which with the barn was soon consumed about 80 tons 'tis said. We expect soon to be in continual alarms, till something decisive takes place.*

This brief skirmish was one of several secondary engagements in the Boston phase of the Revolution and became known as "the Grape Island Alarm."

The Sansone Promontory just ahead provides a fine view of Boston and the Harbor Islands from where the Back and Fore Rivers meet.

Weymouth Neck extends to Lane Beach, and the Bradleys owned all of it, as well as land on Great Hill. At the corner of the present Fort Point

Above: The Grape Island monument.

Below: Sansone Point, Webb State Park.

Road at Lane Beach there was once a hotel where people would stay to take the waters. Nearby on River Street was a trolley station that served the area.

Heading back toward Webb State and on the right off River Street is Back River Road. There stood a dock where ships from Boston and as far away as Canada unloaded goods, especially when the ironworks was operating at the other end of the Weymouth Back River. Where the houses are now on that side of River Street there was once a farm that grew food for the workers at the fertilizer plant. Dairy cows were kept, too, and a garage on Back River Road was converted from the barn that once housed them.

There was also a school for the children of the workers—most of them Polish immigrants—on the other side of River Street not far from Cliff Street, and there was housing for the workers near Back River in what is now Webb State.

The oldest house on Weymouth Neck is the 1868 Second Empire house on Caldwell Street. The house was there before the street and had to be repositioned when the street was built. It was owned by a liquor merchant from Boston, who apparently spent summers on the Neck, as many others did.

A final story is more recent and has to do with winter. During the Blizzard of '78 a pregnant woman, Mary Kenney, was trapped in her home on Fort Point without electricity and with no way to get out as her moment of delivery drew closer. Spray from Fore River was coating the roof with ice. She had no portable radio and didn't know the extent of the storm or the forecast.

When her husband reached home from his job in Boston on the third day of the storm, they called 911 to try to get her out. But the roads were closed, even most of the major ones. It appeared that she would only be able to get out via a helicopter. At first it was thought that one might land on the basketball court across from the beach, and the town sent a front-end loader to clear it. But when they realized the area was too narrow, it was pulled part way up Fort Point Road on a toboggan to a minivan.

The minivan couldn't get far, so a police cruiser tried. The cruiser got as far as the beach, but the driver couldn't turn around, so he put the cruiser in reverse and backtracked to the intersection of 3A near St. Jerome's, where an ambulance was waiting to take her to South Shore Hospital. That trip, over snow-clogged, bumpy roads, took a half hour, and her son Kristopher was born less than an hour and a half later. For the residents of Weymouth Neck, but especially for Mary, it was a storm to remember.

It was part of local history. History is more than sweeping, world-shattering events. It's all the things that happen locally, too, some of them more memorable than others and all of them important at the time. It's also the churning of places and even of land, turning them from one use into another. How many residents of Weymouth Neck know about Mary Kenney? How many knew who the Bradleys were?

EAST WEYMOUTH—WEYMOUTH HEIGHTS

Jackson Square is the village that centers East Weymouth, where Commercial, Broad and Pleasant Streets meet. If you stand at the Korean War Memorial (a gazebo-like structure) and cross Commercial, you may then head downhill, past the Peck Funeral Home that was once Rice Tavern, a stop on the stagecoach road to Plymouth.

The intersection at the bottom is Commercial Square, and the large wooden building that dominates it was once the Washington School, now used for offices.

Jackson Square, East Weymouth.

Rice Tavern, now a funeral home.

Past the traffic lights are two of Weymouth's older roads. Commercial veers to the left past some older buildings to the East Weymouth transit station, The water beyond that is Back River, and when you go around the bend you will shortly be in Hingham.

The other road out of Commercial Street is High Street, and it also goes to Hingham after passing some older homes, many of which were built by people who worked in shoemaking during the 1800s.

Returning to Commercial Square, stay left on Water. As you walk along on the right, you will come to an outlet of the herring run, at which people often stand in the spring to watch the alewives heading upstream to Whitman's Pond. The fish pass through a culvert under Pleasant Street. The herring run was subject to a vote of town meeting back in the 1600s and has frequently been discussed and voted on since.

If you cross Pleasant and bear to your left around a triangle of land, you will come to Iron Hill Street. Here stood the Weymouth Iron Works during the nineteenth century, including a huge smelter that stood on a rise to your right. Two stone buildings from the works remain at the lower end of the street on the left. Both were awarded a prize for reconstruction. One serves as an office, the other for housing.

Just up the street on the right, the herring run has fish ladders that allow the herring to pass more easily past the dam and into Whitman's Pond, which is just ahead.

The streets on the north side of Jackson Square and up Commercial toward the Maria Weston Chapman Middle School also have period housing of interest. Just beyond Madison Street—once known as "Drury Lane"—1141 Commercial is an 1835 half Cape that was converted from a shoe shop.

Next to the Maria Weston Chapman Middle School is a small cape that has always belonged to the Cowing family, and sources point to this as the birthplace of Maria Weston—and that of her famous uncle Joshua Bates.

Across the street from the tennis courts at Legion Field on the corner of what is now Unicorn stood the Lovell home, in which General Solomon Lovell was raised by his grandfather, Enoch Lovell. General Lovell commanded militia in Boston during the Revolution.

Going up the hill and opposite Legion Field, we come to the Captain William Wildes House, a large yellow house set back from the road that displays Georgian features, especially the symmetrical balance of the left and right sides of the house, including a chimney at each end. Wildes was a sea captain and merchant from Kennebunk, Maine, who married General Lovell's daughter, Mary. He was also active in the shoe industry.

After you pass the World War I cannon at the beginning of Middle Street, you will crest King Oak Hill and reach a Colonial Revival house with some Victorian features, like the cupola and the triangular pediment above the doorway, which extends past the roofline. This was the Elinathan Bates House. He, too, was in the shoe industry.

Just down the hill from the crest but on the same side is the notable W.E. Bicknell House, unmistakable for its Greek Revival style. Its Doric columns are grooved or "fluted" and support a portico with long, narrow windows, and above them a triangular window matches the shape of the roofline of the pediment above.

Across the street, atop the hill but unseen from Commercial Street, is the Binnian/Emery House, which is a copy of George Washington's Mount Vernon. It was built in the early twentieth century.

I return now to Middle Street, aptly named since it stretches along the middle of Weymouth. The geographic center of town is at its intersection with Route 53. On the southwestern corner of that intersection the original town hall or town house once stood, and there is also a marker showing the location of an Indian raid that occurred during King Philip's War (1675). The Mill River, which runs between Great Pond and Whitman's

Weymouth Town Hall, 1928.

Pond, was once visible here but now runs underground where the Shaw's supermarket is and can be seen at the intersection of Route 18 and Route 3, as well as south of that.

Back on Middle Street at number 75, you will come to the town hall. If it looks vaguely familiar, that's probably because it is a replica of the Old State House in Boston but 20 percent larger. Inside you will see splendid rooms and paintings, as well as photographs and other memorabilia of Weymouth's history. After you ascend the magnificent stairways that curl in both directions to the second floor, be sure to look in on the large room next to the mayor's office, where ceremonies are held. It is a colonial marvel.

Next to the town hall is the Ralph Talbot Amphitheatre with a brick wall that has a plaque for each Weymouth citizen who served during military conflict. This area is part of the Civic Center National Historic District.

WEYMOUTH HEIGHTS

The lower end of King Oak Hill is part of Weymouth Heights. This area extends to the North Cemetery and the Abigail Adams House and also up Church Street to the First Church and the John Adams School, both historic places. The railroad trestles of the Old Colony Line bisects the area, and in years gone by there was a depot where the trestles are located.

Just beyond the trestle on Norton Street is Abigail Adams's birthplace, now a National Park Service site.

This building is less than half of the original, which stood several hundred feet to the east across North Street. When the house of Reverend Smith (Abigail's father) became dilapidated, it was sold to a farmer named Ford on the north side of Bicknell Square. Ford used it to house his farmhands.

Finally, the house was condemned to be demolished but was saved by a civic group, the Abigail Adams Society, which raised funds and got the town to cede the house's current location for one dollar. The house was

The First Church, Weymouth Heights.

Above: The John Adams School, now a daycare center.

Below: The Abigail Adams Homestead.

Abigail Adams Circle.

then cut in two and moved over the streets while crowds watched, and then it was joined back together and refurbished. The house continues to be operated by that society but is now part of the National Park Service. It is open mostly during the summer.

The cemetery behind the house and on both sides of North Street is the North Cemetery. Reverend Smith and Abigail's mother are buried there, as are many notable Weymouth citizens, including Thomas Watson. He is best remembered for being the person who helped Alexander Graham Bell invent the telephone and who ran the world's largest shipyard on Fore River. In his will, he asked to be buried overlooking Fore River, which he is. The cemetery has many fine examples of gravestones representing the nearly four-hundred-year history of the town.

The cemetery has a fine Civil War memorial, and from here you can look across Norton Street and see Abigail Adams Circle, the first housing tract development of its type, built just after World War II. Beyond that and past the railroad trestle is First Church, where a reenactment of the wedding of John and Abigail Adams took place in 2008. It is a national historic site, as is the John Adams School across the street from it.

Artistry and Lincoln Square

Each town has its history, but there are also microcosms that lend light and fill out the picture of what a community has been and how it has grown. Such a microcosm is the area around the intersection of Route 53 (Washington Street) and Broad Street, known to most as "Lincoln Square."

It was not intended to be Lincoln Square. That was just another of history's little subplots, and credit is given to (and has been taken by) E.S. Hunt, manufacturer and inventor. Hunt had the great wisdom to write his own history of our town, which he called *Weymouth Ways and Weymouth People: Reminiscences.* He published it himself in 1907. It is indeed his reminiscences and reads almost like a diary-driven recollection of his boyhood and manhood in the smaller, more intimate Weymouth of the 1800s in which his family played a significant part.

As a consequence of his book, we know comparatively a lot about Edmund Soper Hunt and about the Hunts than we do about many other Weymouthites about whom we would like to know more. In one passage, Hunt tells us that in a celebratory moment toward the close of the Civil War, he wrote out a sign and fixed it prominently at the intersection we've been talking about, calling it "Lincoln Square" after our beloved President Lincoln. And so it remained. Abe Lincoln was a big favorite in Weymouth even before the war and was celebrated by the Wide Awakes.

As to E.S. Hunt, there aren't many of us who can claim with assuredness naming anything more than our own children or such things, but Hunt had more than his fifteen minutes of fame, and since he apparently named the square let's talk about him first before going on to some of the other people associated with that area who also deserve attention.

As mentioned earlier, Hunt was an inventor. He had invented a device for sea rescues that was used for many years, but he made his most showy display in the area of fireworks—the kinds used by municipalities such as Weymouth or Boston that draw crowds and shake buildings. His factory of several buildings still stands on the corner of Broad and King. (It is now ElectroSwitch, but in the middle and late 1800s it was E.S. Hunt and Sons.)

If you suspect that Hunt was good at self-promotion, don't discount him as an entrepreneur. In the 1870s, he took advantage of an opening in the market, France went to war with Prussia, and you couldn't get ladies' fans from France for a number of years. A shame, but Hunt saw it as an opportunity. You could still get the fans from Hunt. He stepped up production and cornered the market. Between the fans and the fireworks, Hunt became wealthy. Next to rockets and gold fans, naming a square was a mere bagatelle.

You'll have to imagine the fireworks or think of Hunt when the third of July comes to Lane Beach in North Weymouth. However, you can actually *see* the fans. The town historical museum on the lower floor of Tufts Library has a nice collection of them, and it is open Monday nights. There's a lot more of Weymouth memorabilia there, too.

While you're in the library, you can read Hunt's reminiscences, too. Tufts and all the town's libraries have copies. At Tufts they are in the "Weymouth Room" at the back of the first floor to the left. In Hunt's book you'll see a photo of the author with his full, flowing, Santa-like white beard, and you can follow his nostalgic passage back through the decades of the nineteenth century written in his easy prose. You'll trip lightly over many of those who appear in this story and make your own connections between what is here now and how it must have been. Hunt makes the pill of history easy to swallow.

In a way, Lincoln Square is something of an artists' corner of Weymouth. You might not think so if you stand there, but read on.

In the museum, you'll also find scenes of Weymouth painted by Carroll Bill. He was born in Philadelphia but lived in this area most of his life. Most of his work was in watercolors. Besides his Weymouth work, he has a mural at Logan Airport and other pieces at MIT and at the Museum of Fine Arts. Bill earned a living as an author and illustrator of articles for national magazines.

Weston Park, behind the library and post office, was once the land of the Weston family, of whom Maria Weston Chapman was best known. It was donated to the town. It has some wonderful children's areas. A local artist, Susan Torrey Merritt, who lived during the mid-1900s in Weymouth, became famous for her signed painting *A Fourth of July Picnic at Weymouth Landing Massachusetts*, which she painted in 1846. It is considered one of the major folk art paintings in the United States and depicts an antislavery picnic at Weymouth Landing, with the background at Weston Park where the picnic took place.

The painting is a collage showing cutout figures, painted separately and then affixed to the landscape. That technique allowed an artist to arrange elements into a pleasing composition before making a final decision. Today computers can be used in a similar way, but doing it in that period has been compared to the making of patchwork quilts with the patches being tried in various positions before being stitched into place.

Though Merritt, a member of the ubiquitous South Weymouth Torrey family, is known to have entered artwork contests in town, this major work is the only one that drew any attention. It was signed by her and today it hangs in the Chicago Institute of Art. Curiously, this was the only work for which Merritt was known, though she won many prizes for her artwork at the Weymouth Fair.

One significant building that's adjacent to Weston Park is the U.S. Post Office. Whether you have a letter to mail or not, you may want to take a moment to drop in. The post office is halfway down Washington Street between Lincoln Square and Weymouth Landing.

It was the first U.S. government building in Weymouth, and its exterior is made of Weymouth-mined seam-faced granite, but you must go inside, for there you'll see a fine mural showing the first Weymouth settlers at Wessagusset in 1622. It was painted by Guy Pene du Bois, but it wasn't his usual type of work. Pene du Bois, a child of French immigrants from Louisiana, was known for his paintings in Europe and in America of the "flapper" era.

This work was one of many post office works commissioned by the U.S. Treasury Department during the days of the New Deal, and the mural was one of many commissioned as part of the Works Progress Administration, whereby artists were kept working by giving them public works to do.

There is now a bank up the hill from the post office and across Washington Street from the former fire station at Lincoln Square, but on that site there once stood the First Baptist Church in Weymouth. At one point, the minister there was Reverend William C. Wright. His son, Frank Lloyd Wright, became a famous architect.

It has been speculated that Weymouth's natural beauty may have been the inspiration for Frank Lloyd Wright's famous Fallingwater house in Pennsylvania. However, Wright himself credits his schoolteacher mother for bringing from Weymouth "the new light of transcendentalism, the work of Emerson and Parker."

The family moved around quite a bit, as families of clergymen often do. Frank spent only three youthful years in Weymouth in the late 1870s.

He probably knew about Hunt's sign on Lincoln Square, but there's no evidence that it influenced his work. However, Wright's sister, Maginal Barney Wright, was born in Weymouth in 1881. She was the third child. She later went to school in Chicago, where her big brother was training for his career.

She went on to the Chicago Art Institute (where she possibly saw Susan Torrey Merritt's work of the park behind her father's church). Frank taught her to draw, and it was her brother's encouragement and inspiration that led Maginal to her fine career in art. Among the books she illustrated were some by L. Frank Baum, author of *The Wonderful Wizard of Oz*. Her daughter, Eleanor Enright, became an author and went on to win the Newbery Medal for Children's Literature.

WEYMOUTH LANDING, THEN AND NOW

Our forebears hid gunpowder at Weymouth Landing to keep it from the British, but they may have kept secrets better than the people in Boston and towns to the north and west. General Gage sent his troops to Concord instead of marching them south.

If Weymouth had blabbed about its store of gunpowder, Paul Revere might have left midnight hoof prints along Commercial Street and George Washington might have raised mulled rum at the Arnold Tavern.

Weymouth didn't begin at the Landing. It began in the north around Sea Street, and the early years were a history of that part of town. But the Landing started to develop and became the major commercial center because of its geography.

Some travelers to Weymouth in colonial times were on their way to somewhere else, possibly Plymouth or perchance New Bedford or Bridgewater. They usually forded the river into Weymouth Landing.

Stagecoaches came from Boston and Quincy on their way to Plymouth, stopping in Weymouth Landing. They then followed the snakelike course of Commercial Street to Jackson Square and High Street and then on through Hingham to Plymouth.

Developers built the Queen Anne Turnpike as a toll road along the course of today's Route 53 or Washington Street. They built a tollhouse at the Braintree end of the Landing and another near the stone quarries at the Weymouth-Hingham line. A town with tolls at both ends must have had some value to those who paid to enter.

The American Indian tribes who blazed these trails used the paths of least resistance and followed water bodies wherever they could. These made good landmarks and could also be fished. The sinuous route of Commercial Street along the river and along King Oak Hill makes sense when we think of it that way.

Another route was the present Main Street or Route 18, known as the New Bedford Turnpike. If you turned right at Weymouth Landing onto Front Street, you were on the native-created Narragansett Trail. Colonial travelers could take that to Summer, West and Forest and along Great Pond to Abington and beyond. All these roads led in and out of the Landing and still do.

Boats also docked there at a crude wharf on Smelt Brook. The steel ribbons of the railroad replaced the stagecoach in 1849 with a depot where the tracks crossed Commercial Street before going on to Weymouth Heights. Trolleys came next. From the Braintree Railroad depot they scooted down into the Landing and then rolled up Washington to Broad Street and on to East Weymouth. Buses from T stations replaced the trolleys, and the railroad has replaced its older self.

The Old Colony Railroad at Weymouth Landing.

The Sacred Heart Church, Weymouth Landing.

The Landing was truly a landing as far as freight and commerce were concerned. For much of the nineteenth century, timber was brought from Maine. Mills at the Landing stripped the bark from the logs and made them into boards to be shipped by horse and wagon to Abington, Bridgewater and other landlocked towns over the roads mentioned above.

Several lumberyards stood for many years between the river and Commercial Street, lasting into the late twentieth century. But that wasn't all. That same riverfront area had coal and grain handling. Horses were curried, harnesses made and a livery service took you where ships and stagecoaches and later trains could not. However, a packet did shuttle freight and passengers from the Landing to Boston, captained by Balch Cowing. Other packets also ran to New York, Baltimore and Philadelphia.

Nearby, in the "village" as it was often called, were a blacksmith, a wheelwright, a paint shop, a bakery, two milliners, two general stores and an almshouse, where paupers were cared for. People seldom had to go anywhere else.

In the Weymouth Landing district, many had boot or shoe shops downtown or in their houses. Sometimes they had both. People living in houses on the south (or Washington Street) side of the business district lived upstairs and used the ground floor for business, often shoemaking.

These shoe shops made mostly hand-sewn footwear for local folks. When Landing men signed up to fight in the Civil War (1861) most were listed as shoemakers. "Weymouth" meant quality in shoes and boots everywhere. These shops later closed when others in East and South Weymouth combined into large factories.

Let's fill that picture out a little and try to overlay an image of the past onto today's streets. We'll pause at Washington Square, the intersection of Washington, Commercial and Front Streets. If we stand on the traffic island, watching the traffic inch up the Washington Street incline, we can see the replacement for Sacred Heart Church. Just up the hill on Washington is the post office and to our right is Front Street, with many fine old homes built by those who owned businesses in the Landing. The intersection is crowded, but it is wider than it once was because they removed a building from that area where the little park is located.

Let's put it back for the moment in your mind's eye. The Tufts Library was a large red brick building with turrets like dunce caps on the corners. The children of Cotton Tufts Jr. donated it. The store that he and his partner James Whittemore ran on this site also served as a post office and lending library—truly one-stop shopping.

To the left of the library, and chummily close to it, stood the Wales Hotel, a three-story wooden structure with a slate mansard roof and a wide portico at the front entrance. The hotel served as a stagecoach stop and served people whose ships docked at the landing and, later, those who arrived by railroad. A new parish house for Sacred Heart Church was later built on the foundation.

Like the hotel, the Francis Cowing House next in line on that side of the street was built by shipwright Samuel Arnold Jr. It was a real beauty—an impressive brick mansion designed by famed Boston architect Charles Bulfinch. Sacred Heart School occupies the land now.

Across the street was the Arnold Tavern. It was here that the Committee of Correspondence for Weymouth and nine other towns met during 1775 and where gunpowder was stored. Stagecoach passengers and hotel guests would often repair to this tavern to rid their throats of the dust of the road. Unhappily it was demolished

The Cowing House doorway (Bulfinch design).

in 1927, replaced by a business block that included a movie theatre. These buildings, too, bit the dust in 1961.

Located where the traffic island in Washington Square now sits, there stood a horse trough, and to your right, on the Washington Street side of the business area, a row of elms once stood in front of houses that had businesses on their ground floors.

Before Sacred Heart dominated the area, other churches played major roles. Union Congregational Church (now of Weymouth and Braintree) actually floated here intact from Boston by boat to be placed like a toy on the Braintree side of the landing from 1804 until 1897; however, an ember from a passing train set it afire. People from the two towns worshiped together, just as they've shared the Landing since long ago. After the blaze, it was rebuilt nearby.

Thomas Watson, owner of Fore River Shipyard at the time, rescued items from the church, though he did not regularly attend. His farm was just up Quincy Avenue on the Braintree side, but the Landing was his family's shopping area. He received his mail in Weymouth and sometimes mentioned in his letters that he was looking forward to coming home to Weymouth.

Colonel Minot Thayer, who entertained both Daniel Webster and John Quincy Adams, earlier owned the farm that Watson bought. When Adams spoke at Union Church advocating citizens' right of petition, a parade that included the South Weymouth band accompanied him from the Thayer Farm down to the Landing and the church.

Liberal causes always got a good hearing in the Landing, even at a time when abolitionists were threatened and harassed in freedom-loving Boston by those whose commercial interests lie with leaving slavery alone. The aptly named Liberty Hall was filled with Weymouthites who wanted to listen to notables such as William Lloyd Garrison, Wendell Phillips and former slave Frederick Douglass. Those worthies had to watch their steps in Boston.

At the Universalist Church (located where Sacred Heart's parking lot is now) Olympia Brown became the first female pastor of a regular congregation in the United States. She was also a pioneer in the women's rights movement, as was the abolitionist Maria Weston Chapman. Her father, Captain Warren Weston, had extensive real estate holdings. The Westons were related to the Cowings and to Joshua Bates, the well-known London stockbroker and benefactor of the Boston Public Library. The Weston land occupied a large part of the huge wedge of land along Washington Street and Broad and extending to parts of Front Street.

Much of that land is still vacant, as it is now Weston Park, donated to the town. But the Weston home was located on Washington Street close to where the post office now stands. Maria Weston Chapman spent her later years there and died in the house.

Weymouth Landing has played and continues to play a central role in Weymouth's evolution.

SOUTH WEYMOUTH NAVAL AIR STATION

The large section of South Weymouth once known as the South Weymouth Naval Air Station has gone through a fascinating history and seems to have a glittering future ahead of it. Let's look at the history "backward" by talking about what's happened lately and then looking at what came before.

In June 2009, news broke that the former air base would become home to a movie studio, an announcement that gave a new shot of hope to the area now known as "Southfield."

The California-based International Studio Group plans to build a $147 million motion picture studio on thirty acres of the former South Weymouth Naval Air Station (SWNAS). The complex will be 600,000 square feet and will be used to produce movies, TV shows, video games and other projects. It will all become part of "Southfield," a mini-city being built on the closed air base that expects to include more than 2,800 housing units, a golf course, stores and offices.

The area began as nearly 1,300 acres of undeveloped land in a rural setting. It was an area of rock, woods and swamps. This piece of land was not located on the coast, next to a large population or on a major highway. But more than seventy years ago, sharp eyes had already found it. In 1938, this land had already been surveyed for a proposed municipal airport. Curiously, when the base closed in 1997 there was a lot of discussion about the best use for the land, and one of the favorite suggestions was a municipal airport. It was big, it was flat…it was perfect. But that was not to be, not in 1938 nor in 1998.

In September 1941, three months before most people had ever heard of the words "Pearl Harbor," it was the military that was doing the looking. More than a year earlier, Congress had passed President Franklin

D. Roosevelt's "10,000 Plane Program." It was FDR's attempt to get a reluctant country to defend itself in what he saw as an inevitable war. Our defenses were sadly out of date, and we would have been vulnerable to attack if one were to come within the next few years.

An outgrowth of that act was the navy's "Lighter-Than-Air" (LTA) Program headed by Captain Charles Rosendahl. Rosendahl wanted a location from which the East Coast could be patrolled by air against submarine operations. The Nazi's World War II U-boat campaign had been extremely effective against the British and in sinking ships headed to England from the United States with needed supplies. America was trying to supply the British, but German submarines were sinking so many ships that if they could not be stopped, the Germans seemed likely to win the war.

Several possible sites for the LTA base were considered, but South Weymouth was easily the best. Though it was within a metropolitan area, it was not a congested area, and it was close to the ocean while still a few miles inland. That made it fairly safe from naval bombardment. The government invested heavily and built quickly.

The United States was spending lots of money on the war effort, but the $6 million spent on South Weymouth was the largest amount spent on construction in the region. Although it was flatland, it was typical New England, and they had to remove outcrops of rocks and boulders and also had to fill in marshes and fill in large sections of the land.

In just over six months, on March 1, 1942, it opened. That kind of speed of operation and ability to overcome red tape and obstacles was typical of the nation during World War II, when we went from a state of unpreparedness to the world's greatest military power with remarkable rapidity.

On March 1, 1942, CDR Frederick S. Sachse took control as the first commanding officer. NAS South Weymouth had a unique mix of aircraft. It would be one of only a handful of bases nationwide to have fixed-wing propellers, fixed-wing jets, helicopters and LTA blimps and balloon-type aircraft stationed at the same location at the same time.

Best remembered are the blimps. They were built, repaired, housed and operated from South Weymouth. There were only eight of them, Squadron ZP-11 airships. They were there to patrol the north Atlantic and escort merchant ships across the Atlantic to England, Europe and sometimes the Mediterranean Sea to protect against attack by Axis submarines, and they did a fantastic job of it.

Blimps and hangar at South Weymouth.

Look at the numbers. Merchant ships were being sunk in the *thousands*. Right off our East Coast, 454 were sunk in 1942. Many of these were sunk within the sight of swimmers on American beaches during daylight hours. But as the LTA began to escort convoys of merchant ships, the number of sinkings plunged sharply. In 1943, the first full year of LTA operations, the number was down to 65. In the following two years it dropped to 8 and then 3 as the war ended. No ship escorted by a blimp was ever sunk.

K-class blimps carried depth bombs, underwater detection equipment and radar that could detect a hostile ship from ninety miles distant. When at Weymouth they were housed in two huge hangars, one of timber and the other built of steel. Hangar I, the largest of its type ever built, was roughly one thousand feet long, two hundred feet high and one hundred feet wide.

The facility was closed at the end of World War II but reopened in 1953 as a Naval Air Station for aviation training, taking on some of the functions previously handled at Squantum. At that time $5 million of new construction took place. SOWEY NAS, as it was designated, performed tasks such as aircraft maintenance, refueling, personnel training and housing and administrative support services. The last blimp flight took place in 1961.

From biplanes to blimps, South Weymouth saw it all. The first aircraft stationed at South Weymouth in 1942 was a Goodyear ZNP-K blimp. The last were the C-130T Hercules and the P-3C Orion. In all, more than eighty varieties of aircraft called this home, including Sea King helicopters and A-4 Skyhawk fighters.

One of the blimps, built by Goodyear, flew from South Weymouth to Europe and Africa and then back across the Atlantic landing in sunny Key West, Florida, after eleven days without landing or refueling—a feat that may be held up against the light stage of Steve Fossett's sixty-seven-hour-flight (around the world without refueling), which even in 2005 grabbed headlines.

The aircraft of South Weymouth and elsewhere were on stage annually after World War II and for many years, when crowds of over 100,000 flocked to Weymouth for the magnificent air shows that allowed on-ground inspections, flights and the spectacular performances of groups like the Golden Knights and the Blue Angels.

In the 1950s, the base had two paved runways—one running north–south, the other east–west—to support fixed-wing jet aircraft. The second runway extended beyond Union Street but took some houses and closed the street. The runways were 6,000 and 7,000 feet long. In comparison, Logan's five runways run from 2,550 to 10,080 feet, Hanscom in Bedford has two of 7,000 and 5,000, and none of the airports at Hyannis, Provincetown, Plymouth, New Bedford, Taunton, Nantucket and others exceeds 6,000 feet. Most are quite a bit smaller.

From the end of World War II until 1970, SWNAS provided support for carrier-based anti-submarine warfare and transport units. In 1970, the anti-submarine warfare and transport units were either deactivated or transferred off site. In 1973, Helicopter Anti-Submarine Squadron 92 (VP-92) was commissioned and stationed at SWNAS. That same year, the Marine Air Reserve Training Detachment and a Marine Air Reserve Group were stationed at SWNAS.

In 1971, the navy leased five and a half acres to the Coast Guard to use for buoy maintenance. During the first war with Iraq in 1991, the base was used for support, and more recently it was used to train units for overseas assignment.

In 1972, as Weymouth celebrated its 350th anniversary, the air base celebrated its 30th year of existence. New facilities continued to be built on the base, and in 1987, following the death of a boy at the White Street Gate, a new gate at Route 18 was opened.

In 1996, the last air show drew over 100,000 in what was called the base's "Blue Farewell to Boston." The airfield officially closed on September 30, 1997, after fifty-five years of military service. A few months before the twice-deferred closure notice, a contract had been signed to build a new control tower. New England thrift required that it indeed be built, and it was, but it was never equipped and remained empty.

Also built and meant to last was the Medal of Honor memorial establishing a nexus between Weymouth and the U.S. military, a connection recently drawn into focus by naming the nearby Union Street School the Thomas Hamilton School after the Medal of Honor recipient. In all of America, only Weymouth has had five such heroes. All have schools named for them.

Now, with the widening of Route 18 and the growth of medical facilities nearby, South Weymouth and its former air base face a different kind of future.

SOUTH WEYMOUTH

For many years, South Weymouth changed less than other parts of town, but that is no longer true. While the focus remains the "village" of Columbian Square, that focus has been widening.

Columbian Square, where Pleasant and Union Streets meet Columbian, features a number of low-rise buildings, some of which are historic or of architectural significance like the Fogg Library and Fogg Building. Currently undergoing repairs, the Renaissance-style library is a marvel of artwork inside and out.

Also built by the civic-minded Fogg family is the Fogg Building or "Opera House" located across Columbian Street from Weymouth's first library. Its style is Romanesque in the mode of Boston architect H.H. Richardson, who designed Trinity Church in Copley Square. Built in 1888 to be an opera house, it had a hall on the second floor. Now it's used for housing and retail.

Next door to it is the Hannaford Building from 1938, which houses the Cameo Theatre and is a Georgian Revival building. Columbian Street is fairly wide here, and thought is being given to further widening the whole square. But in the early 1800s Columbian was so narrow that two horse-

Columbian Square, South Weymouth.

drawn carts were unable to pass each other. It was known then as Gunhouse Lane because of the common storehouse of gunpowder kept there.

Just off the square is the rapidly expanding South Shore Hospital. It began in 1922 as Weymouth Hospital when its founders bought the Reed estate on the corner of Route 18 and Columbian Street. To start with, it had twenty beds and an operating room. After many expansions, it now serves 600,000 patients and has a staff of seven hundred people. It is now the fifth largest employer in the region.

As we have seen, South Weymouth became a separate precinct in 1723, and it has been separated from the rest of town, first by distance and more recently by the physical barrier of Route 3. So it has some uniquely South Weymouth things like the naval air station and the Weymouth Fair, both of which are gone now, and of course it has Great Pond, which serves as a water source for the town.

As much as anything, South Weymouth's growth has paralleled that of its industries. For many years that meant shoemaking and collateral businesses. At one time shoe businesses large and small were located on the major streets. These were not only factories that made shoes and boots, but also smaller shops that made things like tacks and laces and eyelets.

Only two buildings remain, both large ones. One is the white, wooden former Jon S. Fogg factory at the corner of Union Street in Columbian Square, which is now used for retail businesses.

The other is Stetson, which exists now as Stetson Place, a huge medical facility with clinics and labs. The interior of the building has been largely preserved with beams, floors and brick exposed from the original building. The building is so big because of the nature of Stetson's operation. Unlike many of the shoemaking concerns, Stetson handled all operations under one roof. In other companies, work done in small shops was taken to and assembled in the main factory.

Stetson was also the last shoemaker to remain open in town, closing its doors in 1973. It is located at Nash's Corner, located across the street from an art deco block of stores, the well-kept Ruggles Block. The busy street in front of Stetson Place is Route 18, Main Street, while Front Street runs behind the building.

Strangely, when Front Street emerges from behind the Stetson Building, the two streets run parallel for awhile and then merge, so we have the unusual situation of the houses on the right side being on Front Street, and the left on Main.

This is a stretch of mostly very old houses. However, the newly widened Main Street, running from here south to the hospital and beyond, is becoming more and more a cluster of medical offices and facilities, providing a new texture to this part of South Weymouth.

When you reach the intersection with Pleasant and Pond Streets, you are in Independence Square. The building on the left is the former Oddfellows Hall, which was also once a shoemaking factory. At one time, public offenders were placed in the stocks that stood in the dusty street in front of this building to expose them to public shame and ridicule.

If you turn right onto Pond you will come to the Alfred Tirrell House at number 11 with its two chimneys and fanlights. Alfred was one of many brothers in the shoe industry. Farther down at number 21 is another Italianate-style house. It belonged to the Civil War general James L. Bates. This sits across from an 1870 Second Empire home. All three are from about the same period, yet you will find an interesting mix of residential architecture in this area.

Another part of South Weymouth that remains mostly residential and has many homes built in the heyday of shoemaking is Union Street, which runs south from Columbian Square and on into Rockland. Several shoe and boot factories once operated nearby. South Weymouth was at last the mainstay of the shoe industry. It still has many homes dating from the busiest shoemaking period and some that are older. A lot of them are located on Union Street, which has many homes of Civil War vintage and some that go back to the 1600s.

Back in Columbian Square, as you look around, you are likely to perceive a small-town feeling that comes from its low-rise but impressive buildings and the openness of the street plan. If you lived on Union Street one hundred years ago and walked to work through this square, you would have seen many of the same buildings but would have been dodging horses and carriages rather than cars and trucks. Wealth and prosperity came from the growth in this center.

If you have ancestors who lived in Weymouth, a good place to trace your roots is at the Jason Holbrook House on Park Avenue next to the firehouse, where the Weymouth Historical Society has a genealogical database, as well as a fine collection of memorabilia.

The Weymouth Fair was held for many years farther east on this street. The fair had agricultural and 4-H exhibitions, cooking competitions and horse racing for more than one hundred years. In 1920, the fair was hit by the "South Weymouth Tornado," but the fair was only delayed three days, and fundraising paid for new buildings. Still, the fair declined in popularity and closed in 1972. Where barns and pavilions stood we now see modern housing.

South Weymouth, rural for many years and fairly static, is slowly changing.

PART IV

Notables

Historical Footprints

Weymouth has had people who were famous and who left their footprints behind, like Abigail Adams. It has had people who were famous and barely left a trace here in Weymouth, like Frank Lloyd Wright. It has had some who are better known elsewhere—like Thomas Watson, known best for inventing the telephone with Alexander Graham Bell or for his shipbuilding in Braintree and Quincy—but who chose to be buried in Weymouth.

Weymouth had Olympia Brown, the first female minister of a parish and a worker for women's suffrage who flew beneath the radar. It had Maria Weston Chapman, whose accomplishments and deeds are substantial but whose personal life in Weymouth seems to have left few footprints.

Peter Bradley was known for his huge fertilizer plant. People remember that because those nitrates left footprints that have just now been plowed under. He is little remembered, though, for bringing the Arabian horse to America.

Another who escaped notice is James Loud, who invented the ballpoint pen but never really got credit for it. Then there was Billy Hill, who had some fame as a songwriter ("The Glory of Love") but who isn't often associated with the town that nurtured him.

We also have our five Medal of Honor winners, more than any other town. The list doesn't end there. Others with Weymouth connections are examples of how our citizens have helped to sew the fabric of American society with their own strands of activity.

Robert Treat Paine was a signer of the Declaration of Independence. His father served as a minister in Weymouth. Paine's path crossed that of Abigail Adams's husband, John, more than once. When the British soldiers were tried for the Boston Massacre, Paine was the prosecutor. Across the courtroom was John Adams, who successfully defended them.

Later, Paine and Adams served their country as members of the Continental Congress and later still served Massachusetts as members of the state's constitutional convention, which ratified the constitution—written mostly by John Adams. Paine also served as chief justice of the Massachusetts Supreme Court.

The Adams-Paine connection didn't end there. Thomas Paine, Robert's son, wrote a song about President John Adams in 1798 called "Adams and Liberty." He sang it at a party, but the host announced that it was incomplete because it didn't mention George Washington and that, until it did, Paine couldn't have any more wine. Paine quickly dashed off an additional stanza, which turned out to be the best one in the song.

Jacob Nash was a carpenter who lived in Weymouth during the seventeenth century. There had to be many carpenters at that time because very few structures had been built and most would have been wooden. Nash built something important, the meetinghouse, in 1682. It was the antecedent of the current church on Church Street.

Nash built another famous building, too. Six years later, Nash and two other Weymouth carpenters, Stephen French and John Holbrook, were hired to build King's Chapel in Boston. The first King's Chapel was made of wood. Today's stone building that stands on the Freedom Trail at the corner of Tremont and School Streets was built fifty-five years later.

The Pratt Library is another building named for a model citizen, Franklin N. Pratt, who was a Boy Scout leader for more than thirty-five years. He owned a print shop located near Jackson Square. It was across the street from the second location of the town hall. Pratt's good deeds lived beyond his own years. He left his shop and his land to the town. The library that now graces that land is named for him.

Booker T. Washington, the founder of the first "Negro college," spent two of his summers in South Weymouth. His 1902–3 summer home was located diagonally across from the South Shore Hospital—or it would be when the hospital was opened about twenty years later.

The Fogg Library, built in 1897 in Columbian Square with an Italian Renaissance look, was funded by John Smith Fogg, a philanthropist whose shoe factory still stands as a commercial building at the corner of Pleasant and Union Streets in Columbian Square. It had a hand-powered elevator—the first in Weymouth—and stands across from the red brick Fogg Building, which he also built.

Joshua Bates had a great respect for books. When he was a young businessman in Boston, he had trouble finding the books he needed, so he went into bookstores and read the books without buying them until they kicked him out.

When he found out that Boston wanted to build a public library, he said he'd give the city $50,000 for books. He also said that the city had to provide a free reading room for 100–150 people.

Joshua Bates's cousin, James Bates, started slowly but had a great finishing kick. When he was done with his schooling, Bates became a teacher in Weymouth. He was good at it, but he never found what he was looking for in the classroom. He used his teaching skills to train men during the Civil War, and his regiment was considered one of the best in the army.

Bates was a skillful military officer and kept getting promoted, all the way to general. He and his men fought in major battles. At Gettysburg, Bates was wounded but kept fighting. Later, he fought alongside General Grant, with whom he was considered a tower of strength.

Dr. Cotton Tufts was a model of civic virtue and volunteerism. Tufts was an original member of the Massachusetts Medical Society and was elected its fourth president, but in Weymouth, he was part of everything important. He was deacon of the Old North Church for forty years, was on all the important committees and led discussions at town meeting for many years. When he walked in, that was the signal to start.

Marshall Dizer was a kind and generous CEO of a major industrial plant at which innovation abounded. Dizer, who built a shoe factory, had a star worker named Douglas Eaton, who learned quickly. At one time, he got hold of a kangaroo skin and figured out how to tan it. The Dizer factory then became the first to make kangaroo shoes. One day the factory called a Boston newspaper to write a story about it. Eaton took a raw kangaroo hide, held it above his head like a trophy and said he'd make a pair of shoes out of it before anyone left for home. He had the shoes done in "The Quickest Time on Record," according to the paper.

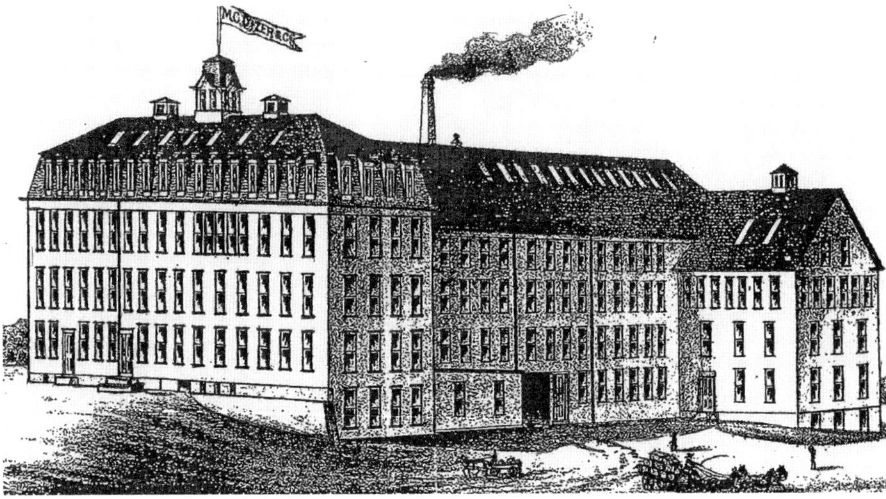

The Marshall Dizer shoe factory.

Another who scuffed the sand a lot without leaving permanent markings was Solomon Lovell. Lovell served in the French and Indian War and also as a brigadier general under General Washington during the siege of Boston in the American Revolution, under General Nathanael Greene in the Rhode Island campaign and as a commander in an early amphibious assault at Penobscot Bay in Maine. Like many American expeditions of that war, it was not successful. However, we won the war. Chester Kevitt's book on the expedition can be found in town libraries.

Lovell, brought up on Neck Street, spent much of his boyhood at his grandfather's house, where Unicorn and Commercial Streets now meet. Lovell's daughter, Mary, married a sea captain named William Wildes, who was from Kennebunk, Maine. They lived in the large yellow Georgian house that he built. It stands today, set back from Commercial above Unicorn and across from Legion Field.

A Harvard College graduate from Charlestown and son of a wealthy mariner and merchant, Reverend William Smith became pastor at Weymouth in 1734. During his tenure the meetinghouse was repaired and plans were made to add a steeple, and then the church burned down in 1751. The pews were salvaged and sold to finance a new church. That worked out so well that parishioners built some extra pews and sold them, too, so that they could add a belfry to the church. Smith served the town and church well for an incredible forty-nine years. Oh yes, during that time he also fathered four children, one of whom was

Abigail Smith (Adams). Smith's original sermons were turned up when the Weymouth Historical Commission hired consultants to make an accounting of town documents.

Smith must have been a good man and an excellent father. His children turned out well, and he was also known to be very patient with young people in his parish, with whom he was quite popular. When he died in 1783 (the year the Revolution ended), he was not readily replaced. He left deep footprints, but his reputation today is largely through his daughter. That's sometimes how it works.

Weymouth Was Wide Awake

Weymouth, Massachusetts, twelve miles south of Boston, was a hotbed of pre–Civil War activity that centered on antislavery people like Maria Weston Chapman and her sisters. Abolitionists and other antislavery people from Boston often gathered in Weymouth, where the climate was friendlier and the streets safer.

The "Liberator" himself, William Lloyd Garrison, who ran a newspaper by that name, made several speeches at the Universalist Church in Weymouth Landing. Many Weymouth people were recruited to the Republican cause and favored the candidacy of Abraham Lincoln.

In those days before radio, television or the Internet, political campaigning took on a different dimension. A favorite tactic was the street demonstration conducted by campaign clubs. These helped to arouse interest in candidates and causes but were also used as social mixers for the young men who belonged to the clubs and young women who supported them. Elections often brought out 80 percent of the enrolled voters.

A Republican group called the Wide Awakes—made up of young, unmarried men—marched in support of its candidate wearing full-length white capes and lacquered white hats. The members carried six-foot-long torches fed by canisters of whale oil and sang party songs. They wanted to get out the vote and also to keep an eye on the voting places. The Democrats had groups that did this, too. You thought, perhaps, that the torchlight parade arose in 1930s Germany, but here was an earlier American version.

Some of the Wide Awakes also formed military groups in preparation for the possibility that southern states might secede from the Union if Lincoln were indeed elected. Curiously, the election of Lincoln, whose family migrated west from Hingham, Massachusetts, brought local fame to Governor John A. Andrew, also from Hingham. It was he who mobilized support and manpower to fight the Civil War.

Andrew, little known outside of political circles, was born in Maine and moved to Boston to practice law, and he had met and married a Hingham woman, Eliza Hersey. They raised four children in that town. Andrew had strong antislavery feelings and was one of the founders of the Free Soil Party, which morphed into the Republicans. He was elected to the legislature in 1858 and easily topped the field in the election of 1860 for governor of Massachusetts.

He didn't look like a governor. He was short and wide with curly hair. He looked more like a kewpie doll than a leader. But looks can mislead, and they did here. Andrew was actually a tower of strength and had great vision as well. When he took office in early January 1861, Lincoln had been elected and Southern states were getting ready to leave the Union and precipitate a civil war.

The friction between the North and the South over the question of slavery and the maintenance of the Union—which began with John Quincy Adams of Massachusetts in the Congress of 1836 and was strengthened with Senator Charles Sumner of Massachusetts in the Congress of 1856—reached tension-breaking intensity in 1861. One by one, the states of the South seceded, Fort Sumter was fired upon and the Civil War began.

Andrew's vision served him well. He could see what was happening and began to get ready for it. He immediately prepared the Massachusetts militia for duty and contacted the other New England governors about allowing their citizens to serve in Massachusetts's regiments. Men from as far away as California eventually joined the units from our state.

Andrew got legislation passed to place the militia on a war footing and raised funds to send it to Washington. When President Lincoln called for troops to protect the nation's capital, those from Massachusetts were first to arrive. Between the time Governor Andrew took office and the firing upon Fort Sumter three months later, he got Massachusetts's troops supplied and trained. Lincoln telegraphed the governors for help on April 15, asking for two regiments. Governor Andrew ordered four regiments to muster on the Boston Common the next day.

Towns responded at once. In "Wide Awake Weymouth," a special committee was formed that recommended to the selectmen that those who volunteered be paid $125. The town meeting raised it to $150. In April, a meeting was held to raise troops, and James Bates of South Weymouth was placed in charge of the Weymouth contingent. Bates would become an important Civil War general.

By that time, troops from other towns had already gathered at Faneuil Hall, and on April 17, 1861, they were on their way south. They became the first unit in the country to reach Washington and save the capital from Confederate attack. Their trip was not easy. Two days after they left Boston, they were attacked in Baltimore by mobs, and four were killed. Governor Andrew had foreseen the trouble in Baltimore and had already chartered steamships to bypass that city in case that state had left the Union to fight on the other side—which it did not.

The Weymouth company went to Fort Warren on Georges Island in May, escorted by the Weymouth band. As part of the Massachusetts Twelfth regiment, it left for New York on its way to Washington. As the troops paraded down Broadway, they marched to the song "John Brown's Body," which was becoming a popular war tune. They also made up verses about a different John Brown, who was a member of their regiment. A bishop who heard the song asked Julia Ward Howe of Boston to write new words, and the song became "The Battle Hymn of the Republic."

Weymouth men fought bravely and well during four years of war. In addition to the service of General James Bates, Thomas Hamilton was awarded the Medal of Honor for his naval action at Vicksburg, and Jerry Quinn of Lovell's Corner removed the Confederate flag at Richmond and replaced it with the Federal flag just before the war came to an end.

Governor Andrew also worked with Frederick Douglass in forming two regiments of black soldiers, the Fifty-fourth and Fifty-fifth Massachusetts, some of whom came from Ohio and other states. After getting permission from the Federal government, he started a regiment with Robert Shaw as colonel, but most black men in the Boston area were reluctant to join. A major problem was that they would not be allowed to serve as officers, and some also feared reprisals if they were captured.

Andrew asked an advisor, George Stearns, for suggestions in filling the ranks. Stearns volunteered to recruit areas near the Canadian border. "There are a great many runaways in Canada, and those are the ones who will go back and fight." Stearns donated much of the cost of recruitment himself. He went to Buffalo, where he was so successful that he recruited enough men to complete the Fifty-fourth regiment and almost all of the Fifty-fifth.

The governor of Ohio asked Stearns to stop taking so many from his state, as he wanted to form his own regiments. The black regiments from Massachusetts were portrayed in the film *Glory* and memorialized in a frieze across the street from the State House in Boston.

When peace came, Andrew argued for leniency toward the South, which Lincoln would have followed had he not been assassinated. In all, Massachusetts contributed 160,000 men to the Northern armies, and they came from every city and town, exceeding the state's quota. From the state treasury, Massachusetts spent $28 million on the war.

When the troops came home bearing their battle flags, they marched with bands blaring up to the State House and presented the battle-torn flags to Governor Andrew. The flags now hang in the rotunda of the capitol, above the portrait of John A. Andrew, the great "War Governor" of Massachusetts.

OLYMPIA BROWN, FIRST FEMALE MINISTER

Olympia Brown found fertile soil for growth in the town of Weymouth, where she became the first American woman to become minister of an established congregation. Olympia served from 1864 to 1869 as minister of the Unitarian Universalism Church of Weymouth and said that her work in Weymouth was the most satisfying of her career. However, there was much more to her career than her Weymouth years.

Olympia graduated in 1860 from Antioch College in Ohio, whose president was the famous educator Horace Mann. She thus became one of only a few college-educated women in this country prior to the Civil War. She liked Antioch so well that the family moved to Ohio so that all four children could get a good education.

While at Antioch she invited Antoinette Brown (no relation) to lecture and preach there. Her preaching helped Olympia to decide that she, too, would become a preacher. This meant that she would have to be accepted at a theological school—another place where women were not welcome. Olympia never shied away from such situations.

All of the schools to which she applied turned her down or just ignored her letter. Then she got a letter from St. Lawrence University in Canton, New York. The president of the divinity school was willing to admit her but told her that he did not think women were called to the ministry. "But I leave that between you and the Great Head of the Church." He was undoubtedly trying to discourage her, but to Olympia's positive way of thinking, he had left the door open and she walked right in.

That wasn't the end of the hurdles. When she showed up for school, she was told that she wasn't expected. But she enrolled anyway and completed her course work in two years. She then had to convince the reluctant ministers of the school to ordain her a minister, and she eventually wore them down. She did some occasional preaching, much of it in New England, and when she was told of a vacancy in Weymouth Landing, Massachusetts, she applied.

Olympia stayed for six years and wrote, "My pastorate in Weymouth was perhaps the most enjoyable part of my ministerial career. The work had all the fascination of a new problem. I had nothing else to divide my attention and my people were thoroughly united and most congenial."

Olympia was no run-of-the-mill minister. Rather than preach from the pulpit as was customary, she walked among the congregation and spoke to them on their level. She was quite a good speaker. In fact, she had studied elocution at a school in Boston known for the skill of its graduates.

Her approach seemed quite radical to many people, but Olympia believed that freedom of religious thought and a liberal church would supply the groundwork to all other freedoms, so her sermons were filled with those ideas. Some of her fellow ministers were not so liberal. When President Lincoln was assassinated in 1865, memorial services were held across the land, including at Weymouth. Some parishes joined together in these efforts, but Olympia Brown made the male ministers uncomfortable, and she had to lead the memorial service of her church alone.

She fell in love with and married a member of the board at her Weymouth church, John Henry Willis, but she continued to use her maiden name. He moved with her to her next two locations—Bridgeport, Connecticut, and Racine, Wisconsin, where he ran a printing business and started a newspaper (which is still running). Both of their children became teachers.

During her time in Weymouth, Olympia also became involved in the women's rights movement, working with Susan B. Anthony and Lucy

Stone, among others. However, that connection led to her departure from Weymouth. Her parish gave her a four-month leave of absence so that she could go to Kansas and campaign for the passage of a women's suffrage amendment. While in Kansas she had to plan, organize and carry out her own campaign and face down hostile townspeople. She gave over three hundred speeches, but only one-third of the male voters approved the amendment and it failed.

Elizabeth Cady Stanton said of her at the time: "She is the most promising young woman now speaking in this cause [women's suffrage]… A graceful, fluent speaker, with wonderful powers of continuity and concentration…In Kansas she spoke every day for four months, twice and three times, Sundays not excepted."

Stanton recounted how Brown and a Kansas judge who opposed women's suffrage had to share a platform and how, at the end, a vote was taken of those in favor of women's suffrage. "All the audience arose, except the judge, and he looked as if he would have given anything if consistence would have permitted him to rise also."

She did not return to Weymouth because she felt that there was a greater challenge waiting in Bridgeport, Connecticut. A stubborn group opposed her there, though. She made many friends and supporters, including the famous showman P.T. Barnum, but she finally left there, her next parish being a rundown church in Racine, Wisconsin.

It's not surprising that her parishes were often in financial or spiritual need. They couldn't afford to hire a male minister. Typically, she whipped them into shape, and when they were able to, they hired a male.

After nine years in Racine, she felt that she had rebuilt the parish and decided to leave full-time ministerial work to become an activist for women's rights. Again her husband supported both her and her new role.

Olympia became vice-president of the National Woman Suffrage Association and promoted reforms that would help women, particularly in the area of education.

When the U.S. Constitution gave women the right to vote, Olympia Brown then dedicated herself to promoting world peace. She was a founding member of the Women's International League for Peace and Freedom.

In 1920, she was one of only a few early workers for women's suffrage still living and able to vote in the first presidential election open to female voters. She was eighty-five years old at the time. She died in Baltimore at age ninety-one.

The Unitarian-Universalist Church, Bicknell Square.

In 1975, Racine, Wisconsin, was getting ready to rename an elementary school. A committee from the church submitted her name, but when three finalists were announced, her name was not among them. That did not stop the women who supported her. They got everyone connected with the church to campaign on her behalf, and the final vote of the school board was to unanimously name the school the Olympia Brown Elementary School. There is also an Olympia Brown Church in Racine.

The church in Weymouth for which she was minister was succeeded by the Unitarian-Universalism Church of Weymouth in Bicknell Square.

ABIGAIL ADAMS, FREE THINKER

Weymouth's best-known citizen is Abigail Adams, though her fame commonly comes from the fact that she was the first woman to be both the wife of a president and the mother of another. Those are singular things, but Abigail was an outstanding person in her own right, and her time with her family in Weymouth surely contributed to that. When we speak of American women who blazed new trails for those who followed, Abigail certainly heads the list.

Born on November 11, 1744, no more than three hundred feet from the present location of the homestead, in what was then a town of about two thousand, Abigail was raised by an exceptional Weymouth family, and they certainly had a lot to do with the person she became.

Her father, the Reverend William Smith of Charlestown, would have been a prominent person in town, even if he had never had children. Smith was the son of a wealthy Boston merchant. His father and his grandfather had both graduated from Harvard, and he did, too.

When Reverend Smith became a minister, he was one of the few who had a college education. He took the position in Weymouth and served longer than anyone would—forty-nine years as minister of the First Church in Weymouth. During that time he saw his parish through many crises.

Abigail was also from a good family on her mother's side. Elizabeth Quincy Smith also was descended from prominent and wealthy New Englanders, these from a part of Quincy called Mount Wollaston.

Her parents provided different influences, and these seem to have worked well together. Mrs. Smith was a pious person and very strict with her children, so much so that she was probably overprotective and certainly did not nurture the creative and adventurous sparks that she would have discovered in Abigail had she been interested in finding them. Abigail learned from her mother to accept whatever life brought them. Marriage and motherhood were the chief duties for women, as she viewed life. However, Abigail and sister Mary conspired to resist their mother's overprotective nature.

Reverend Smith, on the other hand, was more relaxed and also more interested in having his daughter improve her mind, so the two parents probably balanced out. For example, Abigail would have liked to attend the dame school when she reached that age, but her mother didn't think that was appropriate. Her father would have approved, but instead he made sure that she had plenty of learning opportunities right in the parsonage.

Abigail and her two sisters, Mary and Betsy, and her brother Billy grew up in the Weymouth parsonage that stood on East Street just beyond North Street. As the family grew, more room was needed in the little house, so they built an L-shaped addition.

Abigail's childhood was relatively happy and comfortable for the times, although she was often sick as a child. She was high-spirited, but as her Grandmother Quincy, who liked this quality, said of her, "Wild colts make the best horses." Abigail would become a thoroughbred, so to speak.

It wasn't unusual that she did not attend school, as girls of that time seldom received any formal education, but her father prevailed just the same. He loved learning, and he especially loved to read. Abigail would often sit by the fireplace listening to her father as he read the classics to her.

He had one of the finest libraries in the Boston area, and she made good use of it. Not only that, but Grandfather Quincy's house had a library that extended the full length of the house, and in addition, her father's brother, Uncle Isaac Smith, a wealthy merchant and shipowner with a handsome house in Boston, also had a large, well-stocked library.

Abigail had plenty of reading material then. She read history, theology, political books, poetry and plays, and her learning went well beyond her childhood years. Reading and listening in order to gather information became lifelong habits for her. She and sister Mary overheard conversations that led them to take an interest in international affairs, read the foreign news and the debates of parliament.

Listening and conversing did play a major role in her education. Her parents, as prominent Weymouthites with many friends and acquaintances from around the Boston area, had plenty of company—much of it well educated. These people were well read and opinionated, and as Abby mixed with them, she became that way, too.

If we wish to understand what made Abigail unique among women of her era, we must think about the circumstances that were different for her than for others. Surely key was the nature of this positive view about using knowledge to form opinions and then being willing to express her views.

Those traits would play a role in her future life as she would soon find out. It was her ability to take a stand on an issue and argue with the young lawyer, John Adams, that made her stand out among the ordinary and quite colorless young women who he usually met. She often stood up to him, and she was vivacious and had a lively mind. He had never met a young woman quite like her. He found himself taking an interest in Abigail and she in him. After a time, their friendship led to love and marriage.

John first came to the parsonage with Richard Cranch, who was courting Mary. A third friend was Dr. Cotton Tufts, her cousin. Tufts was twelve years older—tall, lanky and homely. Later he would marry Mrs. Smith's sister, Lucy Quincy, and become Abby's uncle as well as cousin. She called him "Uncle Tufts."

Her mother didn't think much of this young lawyer, Adams, as a marriage prospect, but she came to realize that his family were honest, hardworking people. Though his father was a farmer, John had attended Harvard, and his grandmother was the granddaughter of Pilgrims John Alden and Priscilla Mullins.

Abigail's father married the couple in his church on October 25, 1764, and they set up a home in Braintree (now Quincy). She soon became pregnant, and Abigail learned to stay home and manage the household and its expenses while John, an itinerant lawyer at that point, was often away for weeks and months at a time.

This was not what Abigail thought marriage was going to be. She missed the companionship of the person who had become her best friend, and she had five children to deal with besides. But she adjusted well and learned to cope with her situation. When, a few years later, they moved to Brattle Square in Boston—where the Government Center is now—she learned to love the hustle and bustle in which she could socialize with the most influential families in the Bay State, read four newspapers a day and keep up with current events—which were dramatic indeed with the events leading up to the Revolution.

It became a bit too exciting, and the Adamses moved back to the farm. But it wasn't long before John became embroiled in the politics and was elected a delegate to the Continental Congress. This time his travels took him to Philadelphia, leaving the farm and household in her hands. She found that she was good at it. She made the farm and household run smoothly and economically and even made a few investments. She was proud of her husband's election as delegate to the Continental Congress and liked to think of herself as Mrs. Delegate: "Why should we not assume your titles when we give you up our names?"

The single facet of her life that has made her best known to us is her letters to and from John. Historians can and do take great satisfaction from the treasure-trove of about two thousand pieces of correspondence that she left for us.

Abigail's letters were special. They were her way of expressing her ideas and opinions—expression usually denied to an intellectual, self-educated woman. Letters were an exception. Teenage girls learned to write them as did she. Though she wrote to friends, family and acquaintances, it was the correspondence between husband and wife that shaped their relationship. Without their intent, the letters became a channel of greater intimacy between her and her spouse.

Letters were easier, too. Just as many people find it less intimidating to use e-mail than to speak on the telephone, it seems that letter-writing allowed more openness for these two well-disciplined spouses than speaking face-to-face. Moreover, their long absences from each other made it necessary to stay in touch via mail. Abigail said so: "My pen is always freer than my tongue. I have wrote many things to you that I suppose I never could have talk'd."

Her intelligence and strong opinions come through in the letters, and John's answers show that her ideas were connecting and that she was having an influence. In fact, the channeling of this female's strong ideas through her influential husband may have been where she made her deepest mark on history.

Clearly, she often reflected on the inequity and difficulty of having to make her influence felt through her husband. She believed that a man and woman shared the task of making a life and that they each had responsibilities for making a marriage, a family or a situation work.

Abigail took this a step further, though. She believed that women ought to be educated and that they should share legal rights, too. She wrote to her husband about educating girls and women: "You need not be told how much female education is neglected, nor how fashionable it has been to ridicule Female learning," and "If we mean to have Heroes, Statesmen, and philosophers, we should have learned women." (John Adams said he agreed with her.)

The words that she wrote to John while he was in Philadelphia drafting laws for the new country have become famous: "Remember the Ladies, and be more generous and favourable to them than your ancestors. Do not put such unlimited power into the hands of the Husbands. Remember all Men would be tyrants if they could. If perticular care and attention is not paid to the Ladies we are determined to foment a Rebelion, and will not hold ourselves bound by any Laws in which we have no voice, or Representation."

John might have liked to do as she asked and make the changes she wanted, but he couldn't. Even so, Abigail was a leader among women in speaking out for the rights of women. In fact, her speaking out made her unique among women, since they just didn't do that in her day.

Abigail never lost her love for learning. When living in England in the late 1780s, Abigail took advantage of opportunities to learn physics and other kinds of science, even enrolling in a lecture series that gave her a view of the wider world women usually had no part of. She described the experience as "like going into a Beautiful country, which I never saw before, A Country which our American Females are not permitted to visit or inspect."

Abigail was also a loyal spouse, often defending John against his many critics and soothing his hurt feelings. During his first months as president, as he waited for her to join him in Philadelphia, he asked her to hurry: "I never wanted your Advice and assistance more in my life," and "The Times are critical and dangerous, and I must have you here to assist me."

After she died, her son John Quincy Adams would go on to become the sixth president of the United States. John Quincy wrote in his journal a private tribute to his mother: "There is not a virtue that can abide in the female heart but it was the ornament of hers. She had been fifty-four years the delight of my father's heart, the sweetener of all his toils, the comforter of all his sorrows, the sharer and heightener of all his joys."

She did come to live with John during much of his term as president. Her receptions as first lady were formal, like those of Martha Washington, but the food and the décor were better. Her routine during these receptions was to stand in a certain place and receive guests. Not surprisingly, she frequently got involved in political discussions and wasn't afraid to offer her opinions.

In 1800, the Adamses moved into the newly built White House on the rutted and muddy streets of Washington, D.C. They were its first occupants. Abigail liked the way the house was constructed architecturally, but she found it cold and drafty. There was never enough firewood, most of the rooms were just framed rather than finished, it was poorly lit and the stairways weren't finished. After all those years running the farm and house at home, these problems didn't daunt her. The management skills she had learned came to the fore. It is well known, for example, that she used the East Room to hang her washing.

During their time in Paris, Abigail had become very friendly with Thomas Jefferson and his younger daughter. But when Jefferson became vice president in the Adams administration, politics trumped friendship, and she came to view him as a traitor, and some of her remarks became known to him. The friendship of Adams and Jefferson was lost for many years, but after both had retired from the White House, it was Abigail who (without John's knowledge) got the two men to correspond once more. Their correspondence lasted until the day they both died: July 4, 1826.

By then, Abigail was gone. She had seen their son Charles die due to alcoholism, their daughter Nabby die of cancer and was pleased with the career of John Quincy, though she did not live to see him become president. Abigail died of typhus on October 28, 1818. She was seventy-four.

Cotton Tufts, Civic Leader

Every town needs a Cotton Tufts, and many of the first ones in Massachusetts had such an upstanding person. The town of Weymouth was lucky to be one of them. Tufts was involved in and usually led most civic activities during the late eighteenth and early nineteenth centuries. Indeed, his influence was felt in the state and to some extent in the nation.

Most people in Weymouth are likely to associate him with the library that bears his name, while outsiders wonder whether he founded Tufts University (he didn't, and he's only distantly related to those who did). It would be more appropriate to associate his name with medicine, in which he was a colonial pioneer, and with local government, in which he was intimately involved.

It was medicine that brought Cotton Tufts to Weymouth. Tufts was born in 1732 in the town of Medford, north of Boston. He did have a common ancestor with the founder of the university in that town, but his own father, Peter, was a doctor. It was clear at an early age that he was gifted and intelligent. He entered a competition in which he won college tuition and was accepted at Harvard at the tender age of fourteen.

At that time, the course of study in medicine, like most professions, was different than it is now. After four years at Harvard, he had to serve as an apprentice to an accredited doctor for another four. But Cotton advanced rather more quickly than most.

Since his father was a doctor, when Cotton completed Harvard in 1749, he was apprenticed to his own dad. When his father died, he continued his apprentice with his older brother, also a doctor.

While still an apprentice, Cotton Tufts perfected a palliative that lessened the symptoms of diphtheria. While we don't think of diphtheria as a dangerous disease, it was in those days, and Tufts's breakthrough was an impressive contribution to medicine, so much so that Harvard reduced his apprenticeship to two years, which meant that by the young age of twenty, he was all set to become a medical doctor and did so. He was also ready to come to Weymouth. The town needed him. There had been a lot of deaths due to disease in recent years, and besides he had relatives in the town.

So he bought land, built a house and set up practice near where the railroad trestle now crosses over North Street near the present Abigail Adams Circle. This was just a stone's throw from East Street, where his relatives lived.

You see, Cotton Tufts's mother was the sister of Reverend William Smith, minister of Weymouth's First Church and father of Abigail Smith (later Adams). This was a closely knit family, as we'll see. Cotton was a cousin of Abigail and her two sisters and brother, and later, when Dr. Tufts married Abigail's aunt, who was a year and a half younger than he, he was related to both sides of the Smith family, for the aunt was Abigail's mother's sister. It also made him "Uncle Tufts" to Abigail and her siblings.

Abigail, of course, married John Adams, who was a good friend of Dr. Tufts, and when she was pregnant with John Quincy, she stayed at her mother's house, which had better conditions for a delivery. That house was just across from Dr. Tufts's house, so it was easy for him to attend to her.

Cotton Tufts was the kind of doctor who cared for his patients in a very thorough way. For instance, he had a number who lived in North Weymouth who found it hard to travel any distance in order to get food or other necessities, so he opened a store on North Street between his house and the corner of Church Street and hired someone to tend it. (Later, his son, Cotton Tufts Jr., opened a store at Washington Square in the Landing that also served as a post office and lending library. His grandson was also a merchant.)

Dr. Tufts had business of his own in the Landing. He was the head of the Committee of Correspondence that met in Arnold's Tavern in the years just before the Revolution in order to make plans for the various towns to resist British oppression. Several South Shore towns met there, and they also stored gunpowder in the tavern to hide it from possible confiscation.

That was not his only foray into political life, however. He served in the Massachusetts Senate from 1781 to 1782 and from 1783 to 1792, during what was called the "Critical Period" of American history. Weymouth historian Gilbert Nash described his personality as "firm, patriotic and influential."

He was also appointed a member of the Constitutional Convention that gave Massachusetts's approval to the new U.S. Constitution. He supported the position of the Federalists who wanted a strong national government with certain rights reserved for the state. That made him an ally of such men as Washington, Hamilton, Madison, John Jay and John Adams. It was their position that eventually triumphed.

Some of Cotton Tufts's correspondence may still be read. (Massachusetts Historical Society has it on microform.) One notable letter was sent to John Adams in his role as a member of the Continental Congress in Philadelphia. Tufts made political suggestions to his cousin by marriage, and in a letter from June 23, 1776, Adams notes that Tufts had mentioned independence and tells him that a committee has been formed to prepare a document for a confederation of states and a declaration (of independence). It came to pass that Adams served on this committee and helped to prepare the Declaration that would pass the Congress on July 2, 1776. By that time, Tufts probably had received Adams's letter.

Tufts also acted as administrator for his friend John Adams, particularly when he was sent to Europe to represent the United States. In fact, it was he who purchased the land on which the Adams estate is located today in Quincy.

Certainly his contributions to medicine were primary among Tufts's achievement. He was an original member of the Massachusetts Medical Society and was elected its fourth president, serving from 1787 to 1795.

The Cotton Tufts Society recognizes leaders via the Tufts Veterinary Funds. It was Tufts himself who wrote the first article on animal diseases published in the United States in 1785. He also was a founder of the Academy of Arts and Sciences.

His various roles as civic leader took much of his time since he was involved in practically every important endeavor. He served for forty years as deacon of the Old North Church, near his home, served on most of the significant town committees and led discussions and votes at town meetings. His appearance, it is said, often acted as a signal to start the meeting.

Tufts's name often appeared in town meeting reports such as the following:

> *Voted that the quantity of fish, called alewives, taken this year for the market shall not exceed sixty barrels nor less than thirty barrels provided they can be caught. And that Cotton Tufts Esq., be and hereby is appointed to take and dispose of the same, he allowing and paying to the town treasurer 3s. 4P. he accounting to the town treasurer at 700 fish per barrel.*
>
> *...Voted to accept the offer of Thomas Hobart of Pembroke, i.e., 60s. per ton for the ore of Great, Whitman's and Whortleberry ponds, said contract to run for thirty years, and Capt. Asa White, Solomon Lovell and Cotton Tufts were chosen as a commission to make the necessary paper and secure a proper guarantee.*

Weymouth played an important role in the run-up to the American Revolution in all its aspects. Dr. Tufts, Colonel Lovell, Major Vining, Captain Asa White and Josiah Colson were chosen by committee to see that there was no neglect of proper arms and equipment among those liable to military duty:

> *Voted to accept the offer of Mr. Patty to the town of the use of two swivel guns now at Salem belonging to the said Patty. Voted the thanks of the town to Cotton Tufts for his offer of bringing the guns from Salem to Weymouth.*

> *Voted that Dr. Tufts be allowed to set up a hospital for inoculating for the Small Pox if he pleaseth at a convenient place.*

From herrings to hospitals, no job was beyond the purview of Cotton Tufts.

In his will, Tufts gave generous donations to public institutions, particularly to colleges and hospitals. But he also willed $10,000 to

Weymouth for a free library. He had only the one child, Cotton Tufts Jr., who operated the store at the Landing with James Whittemore of Front Street. Tufts Jr. bought the Thayer estate at 246 Commercial Street, which still stands, overlooking the river, close to where the railroad crosses Commercial Street.

A grandchild, Quincy Tufts, also lived in the house at Thayer's Landing and was also a merchant. His store, however, was located on Washington Street in Boston, just opposite the Old South Meeting House, and it did very well.

Quincy Tufts willed funds to open the Tufts Library in Weymouth Landing in 1880 with 2,400 volumes. It was his sister, Susannah Tufts, who also lived in the home on Commercial Streets and who saw that his wishes were fulfilled. She, like Quincy Tufts, never married or had children. She inherited the estate.

Gilbert Nash said of Cotton Tufts, "[H]is power was felt by all the community in which he dwelt. He stood before them the urbane, old-school gentleman, the type of which has long since died out from among us, he being, perhaps its latest representative."

The Tufts family lacked longevity, living in Weymouth for fewer than 125 years among all the generations. Even in that short time they, and especially he, made a major impact on the community. He died in 1815 and was interred in the burying ground on North Street.

Joshua Bates, International Banker

Sometimes a person must leave his or her hometown to become famous. That was true of Abigail Adams, who spent most of her life in Quincy and Braintree, as well as Philadelphia, Washington, London and Paris. Billy Hill, the songwriter, found fame in New York and Hollywood, Cotton Tufts in the annals of medicine, Olympia Brown in Bridgeport and Racine, James L. Bates on Civil War battlefields and his cousin Joshua in London financial circles.

Joshua was born in Weymouth in 1788 and educated in Weymouth schools. He was born on Commercial Street, near the present Maria Weston Chapman Middle School. Maria was, in fact, his niece, and there are some indications that she was also born in the same house.

Once he became wealthy in England, Joshua paid for his niece to be educated there, but she made her name as an antislavery advocate mostly in Boston.

Joshua had deep Weymouth roots, however. His father was a colonel during the Revolution and served under General George Washington. Joshua attended Weymouth schools, graduating from the high school at age fifteen. (He has recently been named to that school's hall of fame.)

In the Weymouth schools and throughout his life, Joshua excelled at math. He went from being precise and accurate to being exceptional in the handling of money, and he started to show these skills when he went to work in the counting house of William Gray and Son of Boston, the largest shipowners in America. Gray was a top Boston firm in handling international trade, including the fairly new China trade, which was thriving at that time.

Young Bates was no ordinary hired hand. He was one of those people to whom you could hand a difficult problem, and he'd solve it without bothering you until it was done. In fact, he had so much good business sense that he soon won the trust of both William Gray and Son. But like many supernovas of business, it was hard to keep such a find. Joshua realized that if he could make pots of money for the Grays, he could do the same for himself, so he opened his own business with a partner named Bedford.

Fortunately for the Grays, it was a bad time to be starting out. The War of 1812 ruined trade in the port of Boston, and the new business failed. The Grays were happy to take Bates back. They sent him to Europe as their agent, and there he was thrown into company with the world's money brokers. Joshua, who was a gem, caught the eye of the European bankers and got on good terms with the great commercial banking houses such as the Hopes and the Barings, while still controlling Gray's business affairs.

He became close with John Baring and the two formed a partnership. By 1828, both were taken into the firm of Baring's Brothers in London, and Joshua eventually became the senior partner.

Bates married the daughter of Samuel Sturgis, whose family was involved in the China opium trade and whose nephew also rose to head the bank. The Sturgis family was related by marriage to the Perkins family of Salem and Boston. Thomas Handasyd Perkins (later a noted philanthropist and founder of the Perkins School for the Blind) was one of the first in Salem to trade with China. Their business was handled by

Joshua Bates through the Barings Bank in London. (You can learn more about this period at the Peabody Essex Museum in Salem.) While the China trade lasted, they earned piles of money, and so did Bates.

Bates was ready to retire by the time he reached his early sixties, since he had more money than he could ever spend. He said, "I do not any longer work for money, but having arrived at that age when it would be impossible for me to arrive at any other distinction than that of a Merchant, I feel that it *is* something to be at the head of the first commercial House of the World."

He seemed to believe that he had accomplished plenty of distinction and could be comfortably listless on his list of laurels, but like many people of greatness he didn't realize that forces beyond his knowing could yet control his life and add to his heritage.

Ironically, the War of 1812, which had once given his fortunes a slippery twist, now took another spin. The war had ended about forty years earlier, but there had been many disputes between British and American interests that remained unsettled.

In order to clear these up at last, a joint commission of British and Americans was formed, but it needed an umpire—someone with some international background, known for fairness and not obviously partial to either side. Joshua Bates was American but seemed to be British. He was the perfect choice.

He had to come up with solutions when the two sides could not agree. That meant that he would be making all the tough decisions, since the easy ones had already been attended to. The position called for more than just common sense. Some arguments required an understanding and complete discussion of key questions in international law.

Joshua was in virgin territory here, but he had learned many years ago how to dig into the books and find out what he didn't already know. He must have done it well, for to this day none of his decisions was ever questioned.

This experience recalls for us that, as a young man, Bates had great difficulty getting the books he needed in order to learn the things he needed to know. Boston, like most other American cities and towns, had no public library. But there were no flies on Bates. He simply presaged today's era of the café/bookstore. He spent as much time as he could get away with reading the books in Hastings, Etheridge & Bliss's bookstore and thereby educating himself on the cheap.

Bates, then, had added to his list of laurels, had more money than you could wave a wreath at and was sympathetic to penniless people who needed books to get ahead in life. He received word in 1852 that the city of Boston, whose bookshelves he'd browsed, was planning to establish a free public library. This was a no-brainer. He wrote at once to the mayor, offering $50,000 to help.

Bates was still the clever businessman, and he wanted to incentivize his gift. True to his banking background, he thought of that amount as *capital*, and he draped strings from the cash. He said that the money must be *invested* and that the interest on his money must be spent on the purchase of "books of permanent value and authority."

Moreover, and more importantly in terms of his legacy, he also stated that the city must always provide a comfortable place where at least 100–150 patrons could come night or day to sit and read. It must also be free to all. He must have been thinking of the young Joshua hanging out in bookstores.

The Boston City Council, of course, enthusiastically accepted, so Joshua Bates became the first major private contributor to the country's first municipally supported library. Boston Public Library is the country's first such library.

He must have gnawed on this bone a little longer, for he came up with a further contribution. He gave thirty thousand books, raising the value of his donation to $100,000, and he is considered one of the founders of the Boston Public Library. The first library was opened downtown in 1858, and the main reference room was called Bates Hall.

In 1895, the Copley Square building, designed by the famed architect Charles McKim, opened. Its second-floor reading room bore the same name. Bates Hall was recently refurbished at a cost of $2 million from the U.S. government. It runs the full length of Copley Square—218 feet long, 42.5 feet wide and 50 feet high. The room is lit by fifteen arched and grilled windows, which you can view from the street. The building is a National Historic Landmark.

Though he remained in England, when the Civil War broke out he helped the U.S. government with fiscal advice and used his influence in England to prevent the British from raising loans for the South. He died in London on September 24, 1864.

General James L. Bates and His Itchy Feet

To look at the town of Weymouth during various periods of American history, it can be useful to view it from the point of view of its prominent citizens. One such was James L. Bates, and he involved himself in many of America's adventures during his lifetime.

However, James was no wallflower who sat and watched others parading by. He got into things with both feet and was an actor on the stage of life. Part of that seems to have arisen from the fact that James Lawrence Bates, born on August 11, 1820, took a long while to figure out who he was and what he should be about.

Some people who behave as James did are called "footloose and fancy free." It's fitting that the phrase is derived from sailing—when the "foot" of a vessel's sail is not tied down, it is free to go wherever it fancies. Some people are said to be like that, and James often was. He had feelings of restlessness and desires to do something different that arose every now and then and made it almost impossible for him to steer a steady career path.

Instead he steadily saw greener pastures beyond nearly every fence, and he would rapidly strike out in those directions. His movement often involved him in events that immersed America during his years, and this is part of what makes him interesting. America, like Bates, was on the move and changing quickly during the mid-1800s.

His parents were Captain Elijah Bates and Sarah Torrey Bates, both of whom were from long-standing Weymouth families. Speaking of sailing, his father sailed the packet that ran from the Landing to Boston, aiding Weymouth commuters.

James was not much of a student. He did attend public schools in Weymouth for a time. He also attended Monson Academy and Phillips Andover but graduated from neither. It was only when he reached his middle teens that he realized that his education might be worth something and that he'd need to learn something if he wanted to succeed in some way.

When he was through with his schooling, he decided to become a teacher, and he taught in South Weymouth at several different schools. He was apparently quite a good teacher and very popular. However, he decided that teaching wasn't really what he wanted to do.

He was getting that footloose feeling, and this time his itching feet turned to boots. He joined the shoemaking firm of Fogg and Torrey. (This was the John S. Fogg with the factory in Columbian Square and the library and opera house yet to come.) It was Torrey whose family made shoes in Weymouth for many years. But Bates wasn't satisfied to work for Fogg and Torrey; he wanted to be the boss.

After a year, he started his own shoe business with a partner, Benjamin White. But that only lasted a couple of years before he hired on with Nathaniel Shaw who had a shoe factory near Nash's Corner.

But shoes and boots weren't his only thing. He also had music. During the 1840s, he directed a very popular band in East Weymouth. That wasn't all he had a hand in, either. He became the first president of the Weymouth Agricultural and Industrial Society, a group that later owned the land on which the Weymouth Fair was held annually.

In 1849, young men from Weymouth and elsewhere were headed for California. They'd heard news of the finding of gold on Sutter's Farm, and they were off and running as part of the Gold Rush. James's itchy feet joined them, along with several other young men from Weymouth. But, remember, James liked to do things in a big way. He became an entrepreneur with stock in the Boston and California Joint Stock Mining and Trading Company.

The company even had its own ship, the *Edward Everett*, which they equipped for a long voyage around the horn of South America. The ship's name had a Massachusetts connection, being named for the president of Harvard, who would become governor and then senator from Massachusetts.

Edward Everett would one day be asked to be a principal speaker at a Civil War battlefield in Gettysburg, and he spoke for two hours. The next speaker spoke for two minutes and thought his speech had been a failure. On the train ride back to Washington, Everett told this man, "I would be glad if I could flatter myself that I came as near to the central idea of the occasion in two hours as you did in two minutes." Everett was right. It was President Lincoln's speech that would be long remembered. But the ship named for Everett carried other famous people, and its voyage was well recorded.

It carried a minister, Reverend Joseph Benton, who preached during the trip and published his diary chronicling its adventures. William Thomas had come on the voyage because of an interest that sprang from reading Richard Henry Dana's *Two Years Before the Mast.* Thomas himself wrote two books during the voyage, and James Bates kept his own journal, published as *Diary of an Expedition to California*. So it was a busy and well-documented trip. (There's a model of the *Edward Everett* located in the museum at Tufts Library.)

With all this activity, they did at last reach San Francisco, and most of the passengers hurried off to stake their claims in the gold field. Not James L. Bates. He was left with command of the ship. It was all right. The gold mining didn't pan out. The company broke up and sold the ship to James and a few others.

They sailed around South America again but with plenty of room in the hold for a cargo. They stopped in the islands off Peru and loaded guano—fertilizer from sea birds that is rich in nitrates and phosphorus. When they got back to the port of Boston, they sold the cargo for a tidy profit.

Home again, James was out of work, but not for long. He went back to work with Nathaniel Shaw, but only briefly. He had some capital now, and he used it to go into business with Josiah Reed, and for two and a half years they made and sold boots until the next thing came along: a startup livestock company out in Illinois. James was headed west again. That didn't last long, though, and he went back to South Weymouth, where he opened a general store.

That was good for about a year. He went to Boston and opened a business for a few months before he started a new leather business in Boston called Durrell, Bacon and Company. He stayed there until the Civil War broke out. President Lincoln called for volunteers, and Weymouth was ready (as well as wide awake). Led by Bates, the town formed Company H of the Twelfth Regiment of Massachusetts Volunteers, and he was elected its captain.

The Twelfth trained and trained and trained. It was almost two years before they got into the war, but Bates had them in such good shape that they were considered one of the best regiments in the whole Union army. In those two years of getting ready, James found out everything he could about soldiering and military tactics and finally found a career for which he was suited. He loved it!

He also had some preparation for being a leader and for training his men—that was akin to his skills as a schoolteacher. He had enthusiasm and set a good example for his men. They made the mission their own and became known for their teamwork, drill and discipline.

James was good in battle, too. He understood tactics and remained steady under fire. He was soon promoted to major and then to colonel.

The Twelfth fought at Fredericksburg, Chancellorsville and Gettysburg. In that pivotal battle he was wounded in the neck but refused to leave his post. He also fought alongside General Grant, with whom he gained further prestige and honor. A monument to the Twelfth and to Bates stands on Cemetery Ridge at the Gettysburg Battlefield.

Bates was an extremely active and involved commander. He came under fire more than anyone else—twenty-eight times—and at the end of the war was made a brigadier general. He was a charter member and served as commander for Reynolds Post 58, Grand Army of the Republic. He was also elected commander of the Massachusetts Grand Army of the Republic.

When James came back from his soldiering, he and John Fogg went into banking, and then he became a broker in Boston. It seemed that the winding road would have more turns, but on November 11, 1875, he passed away. His large funeral held at the Second Congregational Church in South Weymouth was attended by his many friends and all of his remaining regimental colleagues. He is buried in the Highland Cemetery in South Weymouth, not far from his home at 21 Pond Street, which still stands.

Little has been written about his family. He remained a bachelor until he returned from California. His first wife, Betsey Dyer, passed away, and he then married Mary Jane Tirrell. They had three children: James Wilmot and Annie Tirrell were born before the Civil War and neither married; and Betsey Tirrell was born while Bates was serving in Boston for a short time during the war. She married Edward B. Nevin.

ABOUT THE AUTHOR

Ted Clarke is working on his tenth and eleventh books as this one goes to print. A historian who lives along the coast in Weymouth, he serves as chair of the town's historical commission. In addition to his writing, he has written and narrated five television programs about the history of the town. *Historic Homes* won the 2009 Massachusetts Historical Commission's award for historic preservation.

Clarke, who holds three master's degrees, was a teacher and newspaper columnist for many years. Recently retired, this late bloomer has begun a career as a writer of books. He describes himself as a "Grandpa Moses" of historic nonfiction. His writing style reflects the years of making materials easily accessible to students and readers and also provides evidence of his love of words and the rhythm of phrases.